# Bullet-Point Belief

Colin Morris is a distinguished writer, broadcaster and leading personality of the Methodist Church. Formerly Head of Religious Broadcasting at the BBC, he is a regular contributor to 'Thought for the Day' on Radio 4's *Today* programme.

Rosemary Foxcroft is a radio producer who worked with Colin Morris at the BBC. She produced *Good Morning Sunday* on Radio 2 and also 'Pause for Thought' on the network's most popular programme, *Wake Up to Wogan*. She lives in London.

# Bullet-Point Belief

*The Best of Colin Morris*

Edited by Rosemary Foxcroft
with an introduction by Colin Morris

CANTERBURY
PRESS
Norwich

© in this compilation Rosemary Foxcroft 2007

First published in 2007 by the Canterbury Press Norwich
(a publishing imprint of Hymns Ancient & Modern Limited,
a registered charity)
13–17 Long Lane, London EC1A 9PN

www.scm-canterburypress.co.uk

British Library Cataloguing in Publication data

A catalogue record for this book is available
from the British Library


ISBN 978-1-85311-838-8


Typeset by Regent Typesetting, London
Printed and bound by
William Clowes Ltd, Beccles, Suffolk

# Contents

# Acknowledgements

I am grateful to the following:

The BBC; HarperCollins; Hodder Headline; Lutterworth Press; Dr Natalie Watson, Head of Publishing, Methodist Publishing House; Moira Sleight, Managing Editor, *Methodist Recorder*; SPCK and Sheldon Press; Random House (BBC Books). Details of publications are given in the Sources and Acknowledgements section.

I particularly want to acknowledge the work of the Revd Dr Doris Baird, whose Doctoral thesis written on Colin Morris's life gave me some obscure quotations from his early books written in Africa. And my thanks go to the Revd David Bridge for his editorial expertise.

# Foreword

Colin Morris has been a constant influence on my life. His name was quoted in our house as frequently as Wesley, Watts and Soper. Reverential silence accompanied his broadcasts on 'Thought for the Day', his preaching and intellect held up as a beacon of hope for the Christian faith. His television series and accompanying book, *God-in-a-Box*, compelled me into my chosen career.

My first face-to-face encounter, however, resulted in more worldly, rather than spiritual, advice. I met him soon after starting as a researcher at the BBC when he was Controller of BBC Northern Ireland. Overcome with admiration for the great man I asked him some lame question about succeeding in the BBC and he told me it was all down to 'wearing good shoes'. I have in a curious and inadequate way followed in his footsteps ever since, even living for a while in his old house in Fulham, and currently occupying his old chair as Head of Religion and Ethics. I have heard him preach and speak many times and he has never failed to impress, and so often I have wanted to note down his fabulous turns of phrase.

Here now is a cleverly condensed version of Colin's genius to inspire and challenge those of us who attempt to follow in his wake. Colin can contract to a span huge reams of theology and communicate them in exciting ways, much as Charles Wesley did, opening our eyes to fresh understandings. I know Colin would hate any kind of hagiography so I will end by quoting someone else – a hero of his and mine: it's thanks to Colin, from an article in the *Methodist Recorder* a while back, that I was first bowled over by perhaps the greatest of Wesley's theological summaries: '*Made like him, like him we rise – ours the Cross, the grave, the skies!*'

Michael Wakelin
BBC Head of Religion and Ethics

# Preface

Over the years, when reading books, I've had the habit of jotting down phrases and descriptions which struck me at the time as original or surprising. This book began just as an extension of this hobby. But once the idea of a complete compilation of Colin's writing was agreed with him and I borrowed all the books, it was quite difficult to stop. I had the idea that all the bullet points would be short and concise, and look beautiful on the page, but of course, in reality, keeping the quotes short often cut into a train of thought or a deeper explanation. I was encouraged by the Revd David Bridge, who saw the work in progress, and remarked that Colin was much more than just the author of epigrams. Of course, this is the case and hence some of the quotes are quite lengthy.

Confronting great issues of the day and wrestling with religious dilemmas, through words written and spoken, have been Colin Morris's lifetime's work: I hope they are fairly represented here.

Rosemary Foxcroft

# Introduction

In truth, I never thought Rosemary would carry this project forward to its conclusion, though I had no excuse for underestimating her. When she worked with me at the BBC she kept me up to the mark, and then for ten years as Producer of *Good Morning Sunday* on BBC Radio 2, she kept the presenters, most notably Don Maclean, up to the mark as well. Impervious to flattery, intolerant of excuses, exuding charm and menace in equal measure, she got things done. So when she confronted me with a sample of the manuscript, I assumed she'd soon get bored with ploughing through my books, many out of print, and tapes of my sermons. I mumbled something vaguely encouraging and assumed that was the last I'd hear of the matter.

I was wrong. It is salutary, even a little scary, seeing the bare bones of one's thinking over fifty-odd years paraded for inspection, and not always the bits I would choose. Every now and then I found myself exclaiming, 'Did I really say that?' and remorselessly, Rosemary confronted me with chapter and verse. Once a radio producer, always a radio producer!

I was alarmed by her proposal that the book should be arranged alphabetically. 'But that will make me seem a real know-all!' I protested. In the dead silence that followed I consoled myself with the knowledge that most preachers of my generation have filing cabinets bursting with sermon notes arranged from A to Z, and if they are of a scholarly disposition, from Alpha to Omega as well. In a half-century preaching career, especially if it is based on the liturgical year and a lectionary, the whole range of Christian doctrine and experience is bound to be encompassed.

As will have become obvious, I am not a technical theologian; none of my books was written in the calm of a university library or cloister. Indeed, I am the antithesis of the scholar; I am a propagandist, having neither the ability nor the temperament to be concerned with the judicious analysis of an issue, where opinions are gravely weighed and suitably qualified by careful research. Most of my books have really been tracts for a time, dashed off in haste, dealing with some topic of urgent interest and written from a position of passionate partisanship. They were aimed as much to clarify my own thinking as to enlighten anyone else, and fuelled by a conviction that what I had to say could not wait upon more mature reflection; I had to say it there and then.

Righteous anger is well represented in the Bible, especially in Psalms and the Prophets, and Jesus too was capable of wrath – 'white-washed sepulchres' and all that. Surely the believer who has never been rendered speechless with anger on God's behalf worships a candy-floss Divinity, a little idol who shakes his head sadly at injustice and oppression and retires hurt to some chintzy paradise above the stars? There are some evils so monstrous that it is pointless murmuring in protest, they have got to be screamed down, using a megaphone if necessary, even if the innocent are deafened in the process. I doubt the prophets always chose their words with a scholar's deliberation. The evidence suggests they were men of strong passions whose favourite weapon was the blunderbuss rather than the rapier. For example, each of those 'fat cows of Bashan' insulted by Amos was probably someone's mother, and a few at least must have been harmless old ladies.

I wouldn't presume to put myself in the Amos class, but in what is probably the longest-standing division in the Judeo-Christian tradition, that between the exponents of priestly and prophetic religion, I'm with Moses the mountain man rather than his brother Aaron, the high priest, and my writings reflect the fact; precious little about devotional themes, spirituality and mysticism. If one can divide Christians roughly into two groups, mystics and militants, those who know and those who burn, count me among the more incendiary variety.

Thus, I knew nothing about race relations when I found myself minister of a white congregation in a predominantly black community on the Copperbelt of what was then Northern Rhodesia at a time when an unofficial but rigorous system of apartheid operated in public places. So a series of controversial sermons about the colour-blind gospel resulted in a couple of books and dragged me into the political struggle for independence. There I met Kenneth David Kaunda, afterwards first President of the Republic of Zambia. He paid me the compliment of sharing with me his thinking about the future of the nation, and from our collaboration several more books resulted.

This was really authorship by inadvertence; one thing after another. I had paid little attention to the increasingly heated debate in British ecclesiastical circles about a scheme for union between the Methodist Church and the Anglicans which preoccupied the two churches for most of the 1960s. I wasn't opposed in principle; it seemed to me more a matter of ecclesiastical housekeeping, concerned with clearing up a historically accumulated mess rather than embarking on a central thrust of mission. So I wasn't particularly interested; it was all happening a long way away. Two events changed that.

The first was an extraordinary coincidence. A Zambian who, it turned out, had died of hunger collapsed near my front door on the same day that the interim report of the Anglican–Methodist Union committee arrived in the post. In it there was anguished discussion of a major hitch over what should happen to left-over communion bread – must the priest eat it or could it be given to the birds? I was so enraged by what seemed to me the utter futility of such questions in a hungry world that I wrote *Include Me Out!* in a week-end. That is not a boast but a confession. It was a sustained diatribe, thumped out, with no thought for style or shape, and dispatched to the publishers in such indecent haste that I didn't check the spelling, let alone revise the material. In retrospect I wish I had, but it would have been a different book.

*Include Me Out!* sold almost as many copies as all my other books put together. Of all my writings, it is the classic example of what the experts call contextual theology, the way one's religious thinking is shaped and sharpened by the impact of the events of a time. So it is worth a closer look.

As a result of my involvement in the freedom struggle in Northern Rhodesia, I had become known, according to the white settler-owned national newspaper, as 'The Best Hated Man in Central Africa'. My church had been desecrated, my manse attacked and my life threatened. I was an outcast in my own community, hissed at in the street, greeted by angry waves of foot-stamping if I ventured into the local cinema. Telephone engineers 'forgot' to fix my phone when it went wrong, the Women's Institute lobbied their MPs to have me deported as a dangerous subversive. It became a sporting pastime for gangs of white school children to hurl stones onto the tin roof of my house; appeals to the police to curb them elicited a bored response that indicated I was getting what I deserved. Mostly, this was petty persecution compared to what some Christians have to suffer for their faith, but a thousand pinpricks can be as debilitating as one bite from a hungry lion in the arena.

I was at my lowest ebb when I was bombarded at every post by the endless interim reports, appeals from lobby groups and draft proposals of the Anglican–Methodist union process which was grinding on endlessly month by month, year after year. Was the whole inhabited earth holding its breath to see whether Methodism would take bishops into its system or find an agreed way to dispose of left-over communion bread? Because I was suffering tunnel vision caused by stress I was being less than just to British Christians who were doing many good things besides discussing closer union. But I became fixated on this image of the priest reserving to himself the bread of life while millions starved.

Then I came across the dead Zambian. At that time, the chances of anyone dying of hunger on the Copperbelt, Zambia's wealthiest area, were hundreds to one against. Central Africa is not India with its wraithlike figures sprawled on the pavements of big cities, too weak to move; in Africa, except in refugee camps, extreme poverty tends to be hidden away in the family and village. So I could only see it as a prophetic sign. *Include Me Out!* was the result of my being confronted by personal Judgement in the form of an emaciated corpse. At that moment, there was nothing else I could say; or rather, I had to say that one thing before I had the right to say anything else. Sometimes God's truth has a cosmic sweep which soars beyond the limits of topicality, at other times it is brought to a burning focus in particular events, and the Christian knows he or she must articulate the 'one thing needful for salvation'. All its complexities set aside, the gospel was brought to a burning focus as I was forced to concentrate with desperate intensity on the meaning of one unnoticed human being.

The hungry Zambian exposed the inadequacy of the gospel I was preaching, and he stood for millions of fellow human beings whose precarious hold on life was slipping by inches while we Christians tinkered with ecclesiastical structures like land-lubbers arguing fervently about the correct way to grip a lifebuoy while the drowning man went down for the third and final time.

I don't think theology is a function of geographical location, but one's angle of viewing certainly determines which facets of a many-sided truth one sees. I could not write *Include Me Out!* now; I no longer have a mandate to speak to the affluent from among the poor, and most of my anger has burned itself out; but I would not retract a word of it, not necessarily because all its judgements will stand the test of time but because it was an important chapter of my spiritual autobiography.

God has, however, a nice sense of irony. Having pontificated in *Include Me Out!* at length about the time-wasting ecclesiastical carpentry of union schemes, I found myself in the throes of precisely the same process. The creation of a union Church in independent Zambia became imperative unless the new nation was to remain splintered not only into nine tribal groups but also into Anglican, Methodist and Presbyterian tribes as well. So I was drawn into the discussions which eventually resulted in the United Church of Zambia, which held its uniting service in January 1965, only months after the sovereign Republic of Zambia came into being.

I was elected its first President. It was the rare conjunction of a new Church in a new nation, so Zambia and its people moved into unknown territory. In trying to guide the Church's thinking about nation-building, I found the writings of Reinhold Niebuhr an absolute life-line, so the next couple of books I wrote, though ostensibly about the Church in a new Africa, were so replete with quotations that they became a sort of 'Idiot's Guide to Niebuhr' – the idiot, I hasten to add, being me.

I had begun broadcasting in Africa and, on my return to Britain, after a spell as General Secretary of the Methodist Church's Overseas Division, I was invited to join the BBC, successively as Head of Religious Television, Head of Religious Broadcasting and finally as Controller in Northern Ireland. Inevitably, I needed to reflect on the theology of what we broadcasters were doing, and that led to books on television, religious communication and on taste and standards in BBC programmes.

And since, throughout all the changes in my geographical location and career direction, I have continued to be fascinated and infuriated by the challenges of the preacher's vocation, I have written widely on that as well.

This excursus into a premature obituary sketch was necessary to make the point that, like the rings in a tree trunk or the layers of a rock formation, the extracts in this book spell out not just the stages in my career but also the evolution and sometimes the contradictions of my thought processes. And one thing struck me as I re-read the extracts Rosemary had dug out. When I first embarked on the RMS *Sterling Castle* in Southampton in 1956 bound for the Central Africa, though my knowledge of the world was strictly limited, I brought to bear on it a most complex, theological college-inspired theology. Half a century on, my knowledge of the world is very much more complex but my theology has got simpler.

I believe fewer things but believe them more profoundly. This is, I think, a consequence of a life-time in the communication business. Any Christian doctrine which is so abstruse that it can't be used in public discourse is as near irrelevant as makes no odds. As one of the extracts in the book makes clear, I believe theology's main task is to make the gospel more easily understood by anyone who comes within range of it. Anything else the theologian does is strictly academic business.

So much for the books I have written; what about the books which influenced me? When I first went out to Central Africa in 1956, I was a long way from the nearest library and there was no university for a thousand miles. Because the missionary's baggage allowance was strictly limited, my library was made up of a mere handful of books. For years, I had to rely on them as the raw material of my preaching and writing, and they did not let me down. As I read this manuscript I hear certain ghostly voices speaking through the extracts – abiding influences which have shaped not only my thinking but also the vocabulary and imagery through which I express myself.

They were mostly the classical war-horses of religious scholarship, such as G. R. Driver's commentary on the *Book of Genesis*, T. W. Manson's two volumes on the teaching and parables of Jesus, C. H. Dodd on *Romans*; and Reinhold Niebuhr whom I've already mentioned. But the supreme theological influence on me came from books by the early twentieth-century theologian P. T. Forsyth; *The Person and Place of Christ, Positive Preaching and the Modern Mind, The Church and the Sacraments* and *The Cruciality of the Cross*. He had a power of phrase and a gift of lucid writing that made most other theologians seem trite and tame. His vivid imagery echoes throughout those sections of this book concerned with the holiness of God, the authority of Christ and the power and finality of the cross. Then I had a couple of volumes of Dr Harry Emerson Fosdick's sermons which showed me how preaching should be done.

And of course I couldn't have done without G. K. Chesterton – *Orthodoxy* and *The Everlasting Man*, two of the greatest works of popular apologetics of the twentieth century, abounding in breath-taking paradox, chuckling with wit and bursting with great-hearted compassion for the human condition. Using a mind of extraordinary suppleness, GKC could start from literally anywhere, the most mundane object imaginable – a bunch of keys or a matchbox – and with irresistible logic derive from it the whole of Christian doctrine.

I love Chesterton's intemperateness. There is great profundity in his apparent flippancy – as he said, 'If a thing's worth doing at all, it's worth doing badly.' I think he would have approved of A. N. Whitehead's comment that it is more important that a proposition should be exciting than that it should be true, because the excitement generates the essential energy which drives it on to mark out new ground in thought. The careful scholar will qualify every statement with copious footnotes lest he be savaged to death in the learned journals. The popular apologist has to take a chance, over-simplifying complex truth and affirming it in a clear, confident voice. If his argument is shot to pieces under him, so be it. He picks himself up, dusts himself off and has another go. Paul called it being a fool for Christ's sake. There has been no wiser fool than Chesterton; he was my idol and the model for all my writing.

At Christmas 1963 a friend sent out to me a copy of

Bishop John Robinson's runaway bestseller, *Honest to God*. None of the ferment accompanying its publication had reached Central Africa. I knew nothing of the television and radio programmes it provoked; the cartoons and satirical jokes, the Letters to the Editor; the Archbishop of Canterbury's public condemnation or the bilious verdict of the *Church Times*, 'It is not every day that a bishop goes on record as apparently denying almost every Christian doctrine of the Church in which he holds office.'

I was able to read *Honest to God* without being intimidated by the huge weight of theological and biblical scholarship by way of reviews that had been unleashed upon the book, and I was isolated from the public clamour surrounding it. I loved it, for its honesty and courage, and for its humility. Though John Robinson faced squarely the problems secular society has with religion, he was sensitive to the puzzlement and anxiety some traditional believers would feel about his attempt to find a new way of speaking about God, of understanding Christ, and revivifying prayer.

I even loved the inevitable theological obscurities which came not from sloppy thinking but from the passionate and urgent concern that led him to write it in a hurry because fortuitously he was laid up in bed for three months. If he had put the manuscript aside to be revised at some future date, it might have ended up a more judicious volume, all ambiguities clarified, rough edges smoothed, startling statements balanced. And the end result would have been one more interesting theological tome, but at the cost of the brutal frankness of prophetic utterance.

I wrote *Include Me Out!* six years after the publication of *Honest to God* and in one chapter I relied heavily on some of John Robinson's ideas about prayer in a secular society. A few weeks after my book was published, to my astonishment I got a letter from him. When I saw the letterhead, I was sure he was about to accuse me of near-plagiarism. He began, 'You won't know me, I'm the notorious bishop who wrote *Honest to God . . .*' It was short note congratulating me on the book and enclosing a copy of a review of *Include Me Out!* by Trevor Beeson in the *New Christian*. He'd underlined one passage: 'It is the most significant paperback to have appeared since the Bishop of Woolwich's *Honest to God*. In many ways, it is, I think, more important than *Honest to God*.' It's a nice compliment which I don't believe is true, but on John's part it was graciousness of a very high order; he was a national figure, I was an obscure missionary.

We kept in contact when I returned to Britain. After his death it was said of him that he could be brusque and awkward, occasionally making hurtful remarks not maliciously but through thoughtlessness. I can only say I found him invariably generous in spirit, welcoming and always eager to learn anything I might have picked up during my years in Africa. We met rarely because he was a very busy man in constant demand, but I was trying to write a book about hope which became *The Hammer of the Lord* and he pointed me in the direction of Latin American theologians such as Reuben Alves who had written on the subject.

One of the reasons I admired John so much was that he was a frontiersman, constantly pushing outwards the boundaries of the Christian faith. But his centre remained fixed. Though highly controversial in some Anglican circles, he was a loyal priest of the Church of England, always grateful that it allowed him the freedom to go wherever his theological explorations took him. And it was through him that I was introduced to the thinking and writing of a remarkable group of Anglican scholars of his generation: Hugh Montefiore, W. H. Vanstone, Alan Webster and Geoffrey Lampe, whose Bampton Lecture *God as Spirit* I found so revolutionary as to make *Honest to God* seem conservative.

The *Honest to God* era now seems as remote as the Ice Age, and yet the crucial questions posed by John Robinson and the theologians from whose writings he drew inspiration, Paul Tillich and Dietrich Bonhoeffer, have still not been fully addressed forty years later. The Church ducked them and, embarrassed at the seeming irreverence of these rebellious spirits, moved rightwards both theologically and biblically, raising the drawbridge against the invasion of uncomfortable truths. As a result, perhaps the personal fervour of some believers has intensified but at the cost of being less well equipped to understand and relate to secular culture.

And it is in secular culture rather than the ecclesiastical talking shop that I now find the greatest stimulus. We are told that militant atheism is on the march, spearheaded by Richard Dawkins' bestseller *The God Delusion*. Religion, he insists, is an evolutionary accident, an unfortunate by-product of human faculties which were once useful to us in our upward rise from the primeval swamp but now produce dangerous delusions. In fact, there is nowhere for atheism to march to. It is not an ideology or a manifesto, the rallying point for some pressure group or movement – simply the cry of denial of anyone who finds the evidence for religious belief unconvincing. But we need to listen with care to what such voices are saying. If our faith can be proved false, it ought to be, otherwise we are complicit in the most colossal confidence trick ever perpetuated on humanity.

Richard Dawkins and those who think like him are doing believers a service by ridiculing the phoney authority and sloppy thinking of bad religion, clearing away some of the clutter of false notions to which we have clung like comfort blankets. They are also putting the God-issue high on the public agenda, drawing attention to central religious questions at a time when too much of the modern Church is genitally fixated, arguing with frantic passion about a passage in Leviticus and the exegesis of a verse from Romans.

The fact that so many copies of *The God Delusion* have been sold and it remained on the bestseller list for so long shows that there is a large constituency, much more extensive than the hard-core atheist lobby, interested in reading and talking about God. Dawkins and his fellow evolutionary biologists have raised a series of fascinating questions whose exploration ought to influence the direction of Christian apologetics in the immediate future.

One final disclaimer. I cannot swear that every single sentence in this book is original to me. Given the books I have read and the sermons I have heard over the past fifty years, it would a miracle if someone else's idea or phrase did not lodge in my memory. If so, I hope it will be forgiven me.

Let Chesterton have the last word about this business of writing books. 'In the end it will not matter to us whether we wrote well or ill; whether we fought with pen or crayon. It will matter greatly to us on what side we fought.'

Colin Morris
April 2007

# ADAM

## Living with the consequences

- Adam, egged on by Eve, did nothing particularly heroic; certainly nothing so Promethean as stealing the fire of the gods. Like the man who leant against a skyscraper and was aghast when it toppled over, Adam might protest: 'I did *that*?!' as he set history in motion. In one hand he clutches an apple core; with a wave of the other, he unfolds a saga of the rise and fall of civilisations. What an extraordinary disproportion between cause and effect! But by choosing knowledge Adam acquired freedom as a bonus or a penalty, and humanity has lived with the consequences ever since.
*The Hammer of the Lord*

## Taking humanity further

- This mythological figure, Adam, symbolises the end of what might be called natural evolution, the great upward drive of all life from the simplest to the most complex of organisms. The next phase is not physical but spiritual, not external but internal, not inevitable but voluntary. Jesus took humanity further on its journey towards the source of all life. He was Cosmic Man, the Second Adam who gathered all life in order to present it to God.
*Mankind My Church*

## Begins and ends in a garden

- Robin Lane Fox points out the symmetry between the Garden of Eden and the Garden of the Resurrection –

Adam the gardener, a woman the agent of the Fall, the tree of knowledge an accessory, death the penalty. Then the new Adam, mistaken by Mary for a gardener, reverses the Fall, restores woman and conquers death as the tree of the Cross brings salvation.
*The Hammer of the Lord*

## Superiority outlawed

- 'When Adam delved and Eve span, who was then the gentleman?' cried John Ball, the rebel priest on Blackheath during the Peasants' Revolt. Centuries before Karl Marx, the class system was seen as root of many of society's ills. And the strength of the myth of Adam is that no one who came after him could claim superiority on the grounds of a more splendid forebear. In assigning a common ancestor for all humanity God outlaws superiority of race or class.
*A Week in the Life of God*

## Sexist Scripture

- In Genesis, the hierarchy of gender is established from the beginning. Even the first woman's creation is dependent on the man. And it is to Adam, not to the two of them, that God gives dominion over the earth. Little wonder, then, that many feminists find the Bible a deeply sexist book.
*Lecture, 'The Unfinished Revolution' – Swanwick*

## ADVENT

### In two minds about the end

- Christians can be divided roughly in two groups; those who never think about the End of the World, and those who never think about anything else.
  *Bible Reflections Round the Christian Year*

### The glorious return

- We cannot afford to neglect the doctrine of the glorious return of Christ because it spells out the truth that what God started at the Creation and reaffirmed at the Incarnation he will bring to a conclusion at the Consummation. History won't just drift on; it will be transformed by a decisive intervention – the Harvest of which Jesus speaks in the story of the wheat and the weeds.
  *Bible Reflections Round the Christian Year*

### The End is Nigh

- It's quite fashionable to prophesy that the world will come to an end if we don't do something about such issues as global warming and over-population. That's good green thinking, and we can practise what we preach by using biologically friendly detergents and recycling empty bottles. But to suggest that God might, at any moment, bring the curtain down on history in a grand apocalyptic denouement is an idea as disconcerting as it is strange. Yet we cannot recite the Apostles' Creed, sing Advent hymns or study whole sections of the New Testament without encountering in one form or another the stark message – 'The End is Nigh!'
  *The Hammer of the Lord*

## An astronaut's view

- Christians possess no apparatus or special sense denied anyone else by which to read the shape of tomorrow. They make a more extraordinary claim, that their understanding of the future comes from tomorrow. That word beloved of theologians, eschatology – the study of the Last Things – describes a process which is the exact opposite of prediction. Christian eschatology is certainly a series of statements about the End, but insists that the End is not that which comes after everything else. It is a way of looking at the present from the perspective of the future, rather like an astronaut getting a novel sight of the earth from the surface of the moon.
  *God in the Shower*

## All in all

- Much Christian imagery is concerned with the Last Judgement as an apocalyptic event which accompanies the winding up of all things, but there is another theme in the New Testament which hints at Jesus intervening in every human situation, bearing ultimate choices. It is a necessary corrective to that tendency for Christians to become so obsessed by the End that they are like ecclesiastical fire-watchers on the roof of St Paul's Cathedral during the war looking for contrails in the sky that herald cataclysm. The *parousia* – the Greek word refers to a king visiting a foreign embassy – is also about Christ coming constantly into everything until he is all in all.
  *Mankind My Church*

## Surprise! Surprise!

- It was not the timing of the End so much as the certainty and the surprise of it that Jesus emphasised. This element of surprise is the point of the parables of the pearl and the buried treasure; it is not the value of the hoard uncovered but the astounded joy of the finders which is the critical thing. The End will be a surprise to everyone and a very nasty surprise to some.

*Bible Reflections Round the Christian Year*


## AFRICA

### First lesson

- I arrived in South Africa at Cape Town on the Union Castle liner *Sterling Castle* in July 1956. I strode down the gang-plank convinced I was entering a police state, and in a defiant gesture of defiance I clutched in a prominent position under my arm, Trevor Huddleston's book, *Naught for Your Comfort*. The immigration officer who had a thick Afrikaans accent barely glanced at the book and just waved me through. I felt like Daniel robbed of a glorious encounter with the lions. The anti-climax was complete when I discovered that Huddleston's book was displayed in virtually every bookshop window in Cape Town. It was my first lesson in learning that relations between the races in Africa were much more subtle and complex than I had assumed.

  *The Hour After Midnight*


### Roll call

- It is fashionable to sneer at missionaries. Consider this summary of events following the arrival of the first Methodist missionaries in Northern Rhodesia at the end of the 19th century:

  1895 Feb: Buckenham, Baldwin, Pickering, Chapman and their families arrived from Britain:

1896 Feb: Mrs Pickering's child dies
1896 Feb: Elsie Buckenham dies
1896 July: Henry Buckenham dies
1897 April: Mrs Pickering dies
1902 March: Mrs Baldwin dies

When Chapman heard that Baldwin's wife had died, he hurried over from Nanzila to Nkala to comfort his colleague and found him busily engaged with a hammer and saw knocking together a rough hewn coffin for her.
*The End of the Missionary?*


## The other side

- The radical Rhodesian political leader, Ndabaningi Sitoli, afterwards gaoled, put to me the African nationalists' case against the missionary in a nutshell. 'The missionary came here and said, "Let us pray!" So we closed our eyes, and when we opened them again, we found a Bible in our hands, but our land had gone!'
*Nationalism in Africa*


## Adjectival judgement

- Our whole philosophy of life here [in pre-independence Northern Rhodesia] is based upon a dual system of values. There are 'good' Europeans and 'bad' Europeans, 'good' Africans and 'bad' Africans. The words 'good' and 'bad' have no common reference as between the two races. When a European condescendingly refers to an African as 'a good boy', this is shorthand for he's pretty good *for an African*. And because Europeans treat 'good' Africans better than 'bad' Africans they contrive by some form of mental acrobatics to convince themselves that they are judging their black fellow-citizens solely on their merits as human beings. They are not; they are judging them as *Africans*. The social structure of our society is

6

built upon the nouns – African, European, Asian, rather than on the adjectives, good, bad or indifferent. Therefore it is a static society, for you can change the adjectives by education, culture or religion, but the nouns are immutable, categories of absolute classification which determine a person's destiny.
*Spark in the Stubble*


## Moment of truth

- The other day a Zambian dropped dead not far from my front door. The pathologist said he died of hunger. The same day saw the arrival of my *Methodist Recorder* whose columns were electric with indignation and fret at the postponement of the 1969 Report on the Anglican–Methodist Union talks. It took a little man whose total possessions according to the police were a pair of shorts, a ragged shirt and an empty Biro pen to show me that this union issue which has virtually obsessed the two Churches involved for sixteen years is a near non-event. The world isn't perishing for lack of stronger churches; it is perishing for lack of bread.
*The Hour After Midnight*


## Feed the hungry?

- At one discussion on the Anglican–Methodist union scheme there was a long and anxious debate about the disposal of the bread after holy communion. When a Methodist layman said the custom in his chapel was to feed the birds with it, a bishop recoiled in horror, pointing out that since the bread had been set apart for ever, it must be disposed of in a special way; the priest had to eat it. There must be a parable in that image of God's servant gorging himself on the bread of life in a hungry world.
*The Hour After Midnight*

### Feeling a single pang

- Because the Gospel is simple, the judgement is immediate; it awaits no final summing up of things. It can be put plainly and in personal terms. I saw a starving man and there was no gnawing pain in my gut, I noticed a hunchback and my own back did not ache, I watched a group of exhausted refugees at the border being herded back and forth and I slept well that night. The theologians call it 'identification' and it is worth fifty pages in the average text book. It's much easier to read the fifty pages than to feel a single pang.
*The Hour After Midnight*

### Across the terminals

- Prophetic movements cannot be rejuvenated by jazzing up doctrines or streamlining administration. If any time is left to them, they are only galvanised into life by the shock of falling across the terminals of Jesus' love and human need, taking the full impact of the one and the enormity of the other.
*The Hour After Midnight*

### Throwing the book at them

- During the fraught months in 1957 when I tried to tackle the race issue from the pulpit – and at this time there was still a de facto colour bar in public places in Northern Rhodesia, hence my white congregation did not find what I said congenial – I learned one valuable lesson: throw the book at them. By making sure my arguments were squarely based on Scripture, I forced those who resisted me to argue not against me but against God's word.
*The Hour After Midnight*

## Hate and guilt

- On the morning after my church had been desecrated, I felt for the first time the full impact of the tragedy of race conflict as I looked at my slashed pulpit Bible and the graffiti-stained walls. This was no word game I was playing, some variant of an Oxford Union debate in the middle of Africa. Here was the shocking evidence of a moral struggle which was laying bare the hate and guilt and fear in human hearts. Even my most vociferous critics were silenced for a while. But, as is the way of things, when things got back to normal, I, rather than the vandals, was blamed for the church's desecration. I was accused of shattering the holy calm of God's house with my raucous and disruptive opinions.
*The Hour After Midnight*

## Reaching out

- Feed the world I cannot. Change the system, I doubt it, but reach out and touch another human being in extremis, that I can and ought to be doing. And doing it not only in those parts of the world where poverty is at its most dramatic but also in the faded gentility of bed-sitting rooms where the old, lonely and infirm die by inches, starved as much of love as the sinews of life.
*Include Me Out!*

## The Chaos-Bringer

- Only when we cease to worry about strategies for the survival of the Church and bend all our attention to finding strategies for the survival of hungry people will theology come alive again. What begins as a charitable impulse ends in a political crusade, to accept the challenge of following Jesus the Chaos-Bringer as he turns

our society upside down. But for the rest of our fevered
ecclesiastical obsessions, I chose the way of the coward.
In the immortal words of Sam Goldwyn, 'Include me
out!'
*Include Me Out!*

## Perpetually hopeful

- There is an extraordinary resilience about the peoples of
Africa. In some parts of the continent they have suffered
one calamity after another – war, drought, famine, flood.
But whenever there's a respite they resume their precarious existence with whatever they find to hand, and with
a cheerfulness and courage that is astounding. In spite of
all its grim news, there is something perpetually hopeful
about Africa.
*Get Through Till Nightfall*

## Closer union

- I realised that closer union between our churches was,
apart from anything else, a political necessity in Zambia.
We had over seventy tribes, and at a conservative estimate, fifty-odd religious groups. So by simple arithmetic
there were a hundred and twenty ways our people could
be divided at a time when national unity was our only
safeguard against the tribal chaos into which our neigh-
bouring country, the Congo, had dissolved. We really
could not afford to perpetuate the Methodist and
Anglican and Catholic tribes as well as the Bemba, Lozi
and Bisa.
*Nothing to Defend*

## An extensive thought-world

- We Western Christians are much better at giving than receiving, at teaching than learning. The historical arrogance of power has robbed us of humility. I know whereof I speak. I spent sixteen years as a missionary in Africa; I brought back with me more of the faith than I took out; I learned more than I taught, received more than I gave. I came to recognise that the traditional African in the tiny village occupies a thought-world much more extensive than that of the average Western city dweller. I was privileged to share a rich culture enlivened by human qualities we in the West have lost or never had. The African people received the Gospel I took with me and by bringing their peculiar genius to bear on it, handed it back to me an immeasurably greater thing.
  *Raising the Dead*

## ASCENSION

### Resolving the paradox

- Christianity rests on two apparently contradictory sayings of Jesus: 'I go to my Father', and 'Lo, I am with you always.' What is called the Ascension resolves the paradox. Jesus vanished from his disciples' eyes in order that he might be established in their hearts; his physical presence was removed so that his spiritual presence could remain.
  *Ascension Day sermon*

### Guest preacher

- Just suppose there had been no Ascension. Think fifty years on from the resurrection; imagine posters outside the church at Corinth advertising as guest preacher the

risen Christ. It wouldn't work. It is unthinkable that the risen Christ should be more intensely present to some believers than to others.
*Ascension Day sermon*

## The politics of Ascension

- Though the Ascension sounds rarefied, it is in fact the most political of all Christian doctrines, for it says that the *man* Jesus has been taken up into heaven, which means that our humanity has cosmic dignity. And the struggle is for a political system which affirms and protects that dignity.
*God in the Shower*

## To prepare the way

- The Ascension proclaimed that it was 'expedient' – Luke's word – Jesus should ascend to show that because heaven is his home, so it can be ours too.
*God in the Shower*

## Part of God

- Those vivid phrases in the Ascension story, 'taken up into heaven in a cloud' and 'sitting at the right hand of God', expressed the conviction of the apostles that Jesus had become an essential part of their idea of God.
*Ascension Day sermon*

## ATHEISM

### Soap-box heckler

- I used to speak every week from a soap box on a blitz site in Manchester. We attracted a wide range of hecklers, one of the most vociferous of whom claimed to be Secretary of the League of Militant Atheists. He had half a dozen slogans about the hypocrisy of Christians, the immorality of bishops blessing battleships etc., etc., which he interjected whenever I paused for breath. He knew nothing of the Bible, theology or prayer. He called himself an atheist, but in all charity, he wasn't so much an atheist as an ignoramus.
*A Week in the Life of God*

### The persistence of religion

- Theological argument and conflict amongst believers or intellectual attacks by sceptics never prove fatal to religion. Gods rarely die in battle; they either expire from old age and feebleness or suffer accidental death – knocked down because they get in the way of humanity's forward movement. And on the whole atheism is a hobby for intellectuals. Ordinary people are rarely atheists because they live much too near the bone and need all the help they can get.
*Start Your Own Religion*

### Life in the aquarium

- Richard Dawkins reminds me of a man staring into an aquarium earnestly studying the creatures swimming around, making copious notes before writing a book about life in the ocean; after all, he is an authority on the chemical composition of water. He declines suggestions

that he should jump into the water and share the fishes'
environment in order to understand them better. He
insists that there are much more interesting things to do
with water than swim around in it. Indeed, he feels very
sorry for the poor deluded fish who would surely be
much more fulfilled if they chose some other environment. Fish all seem to have the same problem; they love
being in the water, and they oughtn't to. If they were to
open their fishy eyes a little wider, they might see what a
joy it is to be a fish out of water, able to flap around, gills
opening and shutting frantically, relishing a new found
freedom. They can't breathe, but at least they'll die
sharing the same environment of those who know everything there is to be known about water except how to live
in it.
*Methodist Recorder*

## Hard-wired to believe

- G. K. Chesterton wrote that when someone abandons
  God he does not then believe in nothing, he believes in
  anything. This is a biblical insight. Although according to
  the Psalmist, 'The fool has said in his heart there is no
  God', the Old Testament doesn't really countenance
  atheism. The believer who turns his back on God is actually exchanging one god for another. It assumes that the
  human being is what would now be called a worshipping
  animal. Charles Darwin wrote, 'Belief in all-pervading
  spiritual agencies seems to be universal.' In the language
  of the evolutionary biologist, human beings are hard-
  wired to believe. So three thousand years later, the
  scientists have caught up with biblical thought.
  *Get Through Till Nightfall*

## Literary pessimism

- During my studies, I wrestled with a whole generation of literary figures who had written God out of their scripts and as a consequence had written off human nature. Ionesco saw little in the world except 'evanescence and brutality, rage and nothingness, or hideous, useless hatred, shadows engulfed forever in the night'. To Celine, men are 'monkeys with the gift of speech'; to Samuel Beckett, they are 'bloody ignorant apes, a foul brood'; to Rexroth, 'Life is a mess full of tall children, grown stupider.' Even the writers to be found waving placards in the van of the protest movements seemed to cry out to a God of Justice in whom they did not believe on behalf of the oppressed and the disadvantaged. Then a change began when Albert Camus who in his early writings had denied God in the name of justice began to doubt whether the idea of justice made any sense at all without the idea of God.
*The Hammer of the Lord*

## ATONEMENT

### The crux of the matter

- What founded Christianity was not the teaching or even the life of Jesus but the preaching of the theology of his death and resurrection. The key to history is not the answer to a riddle but the victorious outcome of a battle.
*'Neglected Themes in Modern Preaching'*

### Effectual cost

- P. T. Forsyth writes that because God was fully present in his death, Christ experienced the cost of sin as only God

could do, but he experienced the effects of sin as only a man can do for unlike God he could bleed and die.
*Starting from Scratch*

## The sequence of salvation

- As we read the Gospels now, we tend to trace the sequence of our salvation through the chronology of the story of Jesus: first, his teaching, secondly, his death, thirdly, his resurrection. But for the first Christians, the order of events was: first, faith in the risen Christ; secondly, the gift of the Holy Spirit, and then, thirdly, a realisation of what the Cross meant.
*God in the Shower*

## The lens through which we see

- Christian preaching is fundamentally the preaching *of* the Cross, even though we do not invariably preach *about* it. It is sometimes more appropriate to preach the Christ of the Cross rather than the Cross of Christ. That is a matter of tactics, not of theological emphasis. In one sense, the Cross of Christ is the lens through which we see every other element of our faith. We may explore the whole range of Christian doctrine but sooner or later the track of our spiritual and intellectual journeying will take us past Calvary.
*'Neglected Themes in Modern Preaching'*

## Death of a man

- A man died and humanity was impoverished; a good man died and humanity was judged; cosmic man died and humanity was saved.
*Mankind My Church*

### Drawing power

- For much of his ministry Christ talked of forgiving love. Only at the end did he speak of his blood, pointing to that darker, more mysterious fate which was to befall him. His gracious invitation, 'Come unto me,' failed. It was not his raised voice but his raised cross that had drawing power.
  *What the Papers Didn't Say*

### An extraordinary idea

- In a human sense, Christianity began by an extraordinary idea taking hold of a group of ordinary people and in essence crying, 'Stand for me, believe in me, if necessary, die for me.' What was that extraordinary idea? Paul put it in one sentence: 'God was in Christ reconciling the world to himself.' That is the irreducible minimum creed of Christianity, the constitution of the Kingdom of God, the theme of that sermon we call the Bible, the power of its preaching, the thrust of its ethics, the inspiration of its sacramental life.
  *Sermon, 'What's Right with the Church'*

### Recaptured innocence

- The vicinity of the cross is an area cleared of evil forces where we can recapture innocence of life and purity of intention. Thus the Victorian hymn writer got it right when he advised us to 'Cling to the old rugged cross.'
  *Church and Challenge in a New Africa*

### No official doctrine

- Not even the writers of the New Testament were able to describe adequately what happened to Jesus on the cross.

They went to the law court, the slaughter house and the slave galley for images that cast light on the meaning of Christ's death. But the Church has never officially endorsed any of these pictures. The important thing is that the first Christians felt Jesus had done something on the cross which changed their lives and put them right with God. In their hymns and creeds and sermons they celebrated the fact and only later built a theology round it.
*Sermon*


## The world's centre

• The medieval map makers were spelling out a truth greater than they knew when they took the site of Calvary as the dead centre of the world and then arranged all the continents and land masses around it.
*Wesley Day – Wesley's Chapel*


## Crusading and crucified minds

• The religious mind tends to be of one of two types, crusading or crucified. The crusading mind is cocksure about what it knows and is unequivocal in its demands; all have heard and therefore all must obey. The crucified mind is diffident, almost timid in the claims it makes because it is always conscious of the mystery of the other as a personality with hidden sensitivities and private agonies. It was a quality well demonstrated by Jesus when he asked, 'Who touched me?' when a woman in the crowd touched the hem of his garment. The crucified mind senses who will carry the cross to the end or collapse under its weight; who will bury God's treasure in a field or use it fruitfully; who amongst those who cry, 'Lord, Lord!' will act to the limit of their confession.
*Things Shaken, Things Unshaken*

## A turn of grace

- One of the main themes of theology as story is the miraculous turn of grace – note the words of the parable of the Prodigal, 'This my son was *dead* and is *alive*, was *lost* and is *found*.' Grace is expressed through the great polarities of life, decay and renewal, death and resurrection, sudden ends and strange new beginnings.
  *Wrestling with an Angel*

## Religiosity

- If the days of simple faith have gone, so have the days of simple unfaith. Our society is riddled with true believers hopelessly at odds about what they believe to be true. Exotic faiths permeate the atmosphere seeking new churches in which to become incarnate. Our society may have emancipated itself from Christendom only to put itself in thrall to every conceivable form of religiosity. It is gone on gurus, zipped out on Zen, mad about mantras, eerie about exorcism and obsessed with the occult.
  *Bugles in the Afternoon*

## Losing everything

- Once religion loses the note of the holy it has lost everything.
  *Let God be God*

- Belief differs from faith in that someone else has done the thinking.
  *The Hammer of the Lord*

## Theology as action

- Theology could be described as disciplined reflection on the action of the People of God. And if we don't find much profound theology around, it may be because the Church isn't doing anything particularly significant.
  *Apologetics lecture – Westminster College, Oxford*

## Academic business?

- The primary role of the Christian theologian is to make it easier for the Gospel to be understood; everything else he or she does is just academic business.
  *The Hammer of the Lord*

## Theological inertia

- If the witness of the modern church is faltering, it is not through a failure of tactics nor any lack of evangelical zeal, but from theological inertia. We have decided that doctrine is no longer of much importance compared with a touchy-feely kind of personal experience. The words of Jesus to the woman of Samaria, 'You worship you know not what,' strike uncomfortably close to home.
  *Raising the Dead*

## Doctrinal modesty

- A strange malaise has overtaken the Church, which often shows up in its preaching. Modesty has moved from the organ of ambition to the organ of conviction. Preachers were intended to be personally but not doctrinally modest; to underplay their own virtues but to display the whole range of their convictions. We are in danger of becoming too doctrinally modest to believe in the multiplication table.
  *Raising the Dead*

## True equality

- Carlyle said that human beings are mostly fools. Christianity with much greater realism says that all human beings are fools. We call this declaration of human equality the doctrine of original sin.
  *Sermon*


## Leap of faith

- Some years ago I did a series of radio talks, *Starting from Scratch*, in which I tried to see how far along the road to Christian faith I could get using only my common sense. I came to a shuddering full stop. The story of Jesus of Nazareth inspired, his teaching enlightened and his death was utterly tragic, but to bridge the gap from there to Paul's great affirmation, 'God was in Christ reconciling the world to himself' – was impossible. I couldn't think my way to *that*. I was confronted by a dogma, in its simplest meaning, a religious truth established by Divine revelation and defined by the Church. I had to make a leap of faith.
  *Methodist Recorder*


## Believing in less

- Too many Christians in our day seem to believe more and more fervently in less and less. Belief is an emotion triggered by an idea. If the idea is superficial, the emotion may be intense but it is little more than a glandular tic.
  *Methodist Recorder*

## Bigotry

- Bigotry is the anger of those who have no considered opinions; it is the frenzy of the doctrinally indifferent. It is an unholy alliance of passion and ignorance, not a wholesome marriage of passion and truth.
  *Address to the Methodist Conference*

## Saved and educated

- Look what an intellectual bonus we get as a by-product of the Gospel itself – for example, the great classical tradition of Greek philosophy. Oh, you say, I'm no philosopher; maybe not, but you have absorbed its key concepts hidden in central Christian doctrines such as the Incarnation. Or what about the religious genius of the Jewish people, three thousand years of God-obsession handed on to you? Then there is the glory that was Rome, the understanding of civilisation and law which was the social background of the early Church; we've assimilated that wisdom through our reading of the Acts of the Apostles and the Epistles. Our Gospel has not only saved us; it has educated us.
  *St Cecilia's Day sermon*

## Lifeless definitions

- Cardinal Newman said of the classical proofs for the existence of God, 'They do not warm me nor enlighten me; they do not take away the winter of my desolation nor make my moral being rejoice.' In other words, we can't turn definitions into living experiences. We can study musical theory until we are blue in the face, but unless the penny drops when we hear music, we may as well have a tin ear. Theology follows from religious experience, it rarely triggers it. We don't first of all decide what a being called God is like and then look around for

someone or something that matches the trade description. First comes that sense of strangeness, of awe, an awareness of transcendence, *then* we try to put words round our experience.
*Starting from Scratch*

## Jesus as sticking plaster

- It is the intellectual case for Christianity which is going by default at present. I am not saying it is the only case or even the most important one, but there are rational arguments for Christianity left unexplored in a Church, some sections of which think that hurling Biblical texts like missiles at the agonising problems of our time, or applying Jesus like a sticking plaster to its gaping wounds will miraculously resolve everything. Not for the first time in our history we must argue the faith against all comers, issue by issue, doctrine by doctrine.
  *Apologetics lecture – Westminster College, Oxford*

## Refusing to believe

- The only way of refusing to believe something is to act as though it were untrue. If I'm not sure I can trust you, I will share nothing significant about myself with you, and practically, that is tantamount to distrusting you. If I refuse to lend a hand bailing out a sinking rowing boat because I doubt it's possible to keep it afloat, I'm actively helping to sink her. Whilst I make up my mind, life has settled the issue. I may hold off making up my mind about the reality of God, but I cannot delay making up my life.
  *Start Your Own Religion*

## The perils of liberalism

- I have always been proud to call myself a theological liberal, though I have been painfully aware of some of the double-think into which it led me. The danger is that liberals reserve the right to believe what they like about God but reject God's right to believe what he likes about them. They demand the liberty to whittle down the number of Gospel miracles but deny God the liberty to perform more miracles. It is good liberalism to believe less than is customary about the Christian faith but to damn as fanatics those who believe more. They find it tolerably possible to accept that Jesus rose from the dead but snort with incredulity if someone were to affirm that he expected his Aunt Lily to do the same.
  *The Hammer of the Lord*


## Faith to leap

- In his volume of essays *The Will To Believe*, William James said that one should always believe what is in line with one's needs. It sounds like the elevation of wishful thinking to the status of a theological doctrine but it's worth pondering. He offers the example of a man climbing a mountain who has got himself into such a position that he can only escape by a mighty leap across a crevasse. If he has faith that the leap is possible he has already added to the probability he will succeed; if he trembles and doubts and hesitates, then launches himself in a moment of despair, he has already subtracted from his chances of success because his beliefs are in opposition to his needs.
  *Start Your Own Religion*

## Shaking faith

- Every morning as I listen to news bulletins about a world in agony I'm forced to ask: can I still believe in God today? Any number of events are capable of shaking my faith; if they couldn't, then it seems to me it's not faith at all but a kind of armour-plated certainty which has lost touch with what happens in God's world. Robert Louis Stevenson once wrote, 'Any man can get through till nightfall.' In the face of horrors like Darfur, my struggle is to get through till nightfall with my faith intact. Belief in God is not always the easy option.
  *'Thought for the Day' – BBC Radio 4*

## Chapel culture

- It is hard to over-estimate the significance of the chapel culture in those northern mill and colliery towns in the nineteenth and early twentieth centuries. The ancient Greeks had the *agora*, the market place where street theatre and gymnastic competitions alternated with Socratic argument, the Jews in Old Testament times gathered for poetry, politics and play in the *ecclesia*, and for centuries, African tribes held *ndabas* where disputes were settled and necromancers cast their bones. Not to be outdone, Lancashire Nonconformists had their chapel where they worshipped and played, sang and argued. It was not just a place of worship but a debating club, an informal friendly society in hard times, a dating agency for the young and a companionable place for the elderly. It was less a building than an environment that wrapped one round like a warm blanket.
  *Snapshots*

## Unthinking brutality

• One of my complaints about Biblical literalism is that it turns the poetry of the Bible into arid prose. The Scriptures issued from a people whose habits of mind and forms of speech were highly poetical, and we must take full account of that in interpreting them. Hence, we do less than justice to the profundity of Biblical thought, for example, by treating a fragment of a poem charged with Eastern imagination as a sober scientific account of the sun and moon standing still. The inspired visions of Daniel and Ezekiel are not railway time-table style accounts of a pre-programmed future, nor are the fevered dreams of the Apocalypse coded messages from on high. Not only does this approach ignore serious Biblical scholarship, it tramples underfoot the essential poetry of faith, admittedly for worthy motives – but unthinking brutality is no less destructive than the premeditated sort.
*Raising the Dead*


## Discerning the difference

• The Bible says things both profoundly *true* and plainly mistaken – do you truly believe that God commands us to kill children who are insolent (Exodus 21.15) or that we should stone people to death for adultery, heresy, working on the Sabbath or wearing inappropriate dress in the temple? According to Ezekiel (20.25) God deliberately deceives his people. 'I gave them statutes that were not good and ordinances by which they could not live . . . that they might know that I am the Lord their God.' We love God with our whole mind when we discern the difference between biblical truth and error.
*Address to the Methodist Conference*

## Back beyond the Bible

- Conservatives are half-right to cry, 'Back to the Bible!' We have to go back to the Bible in order to find out what the Bible goes back to. For it is indubitably true that something was making Christianity and moulding New Testament faith before a single word of the Gospels had been set down. It is not that the Bible contains God's word and guards it but that God's word contains the Bible and uses it.
  *Address to the Methodist Conference*

## Unerring guidance

- The Bible's infallibility is not of knowledge nor of historical accuracy but of saving power. It never misleads about the way of salvation.
  *Address to the Methodist Conference*

## Judging the lowest by the highest

- Unless we are to treat the Bible as the literal word of God, we must judge the lowest by the highest, and in the Old Testament we can't get any higher than the portrait of God painted by the prophets. For Christians, the chief value of the Bible is that from its pages steps Jesus who has been described as the human face of God. Anything we read in the Bible which is alien to that spirit should be treated with caution.
  *Bible Reflections Round the Christian Year*

## The key question

- We can relate the Bible to our time by asking one straight question: 'What must the truth be now, if people who thought as they did put it in those words?' Those are the

words of an Anglican theologian, Leonard Hodgson, and they seem to me to be the secret of biblical interpretation.
*Things Shaken, Things Unshaken*

## Loving God with our minds

- The most explosive religious divide is not between the followers of one religion and another, nor between those who are religious and those who are not, but between extreme fundamentalists of any faith who demand blind obedience to the letter of some nailed-down truth, and those who believe they must love God not just with their heart and soul but also with their minds.
*Things Shaken, Things Unshaken*

## Unvarnished truth

- Why was the Bible not censored before publication like the parliamentary record in those countries where politicians are allowed to erase their more asinine comments before the public can read them? The dark, blood-stained bits have been left in; the arrant paganism, the flirting with false gods, the bursts of hate and malevolence that almost curl the edges of the pages. In the end, only the unvarnished truth is redemptive.
*Mankind My Church*

- I trust we have left behind the days when the liberal's ignorance of the Bible was only matched by the evangelical's ignorance of the world to which it must be applied.
*Address to Methodist Conference*

## Imaginative genius

- The Bible is a supreme work of the Spirit-inspired imagination. Take out of it all the metaphors, poetry and figurative speech and there would be very little left; it would be in tatters. The Bible is certainly not infallible nor is it always an accurate account of what happened; indeed, some of its so-called history is pure invention. But it has succeeded in projecting Jesus into the imagination of people over many historical epochs and a wide variety of cultures, generating the energy for personal and social transformation. That is the reason for its unique authority.
  *Methodist Recorder*

## No Christian politics

- I do not believe we can derive from the Bible any distinctive Christian political policies, but I do believe there issues from it a distinctive Christian imperative to do our duty in the political realm.
  *Things Shaken, Things Unshaken*

## BLASPHEMY

## Believers only

- By definition, only believers can blaspheme. If you genuinely don't believe in God, it is no more blasphemous to insult him than to mock Father Christmas. You might cause great offence, but you will not be blaspheming. The 1697 Blasphemy Act confirms this. It runs, '*Any person educated in or making profession of the Christian religion* who by writing, teaching or preaching denies etc. . . .' If you make no profession, you commit no blasphemy.
  *Things Shaken, Things Unshaken*

- In the Temple at Jerusalem, the High Priest was required to pronounce the Sacred Name, so in order to avoid him being guilty of blasphemy, the music of the service was designed to rise to a crescendo at that point; thus, neither God nor the congregation could hear him taking the Lord's name in vain.
  *Let God be God*

## A very little God?

- When Christians complain that satirists and others are insulting God, they are revealing their belief in a very little God. After all, how much damage can you do to Mount Everest by spitting at it?
  *Guardian*

## Back-handed compliment

- Religious satire is a back-handed compliment to the Almighty. Only a living God gets attacked. When did you last hear anyone make fun of Thor or Jupiter?
  *'Thought for the Day' – BBC Radio 4*

- First century society crucified Jesus; why should we expect a secular society to treat him with kid gloves?
  *'Thought for the Day' – BBC Radio 4*

- All theology, God-talk, is fraught with the risk of blasphemy. A Professor of Divinity is in a dangerous occupation.
  *A Week in the Life of God*

# BROADCASTING

## Disembodied voices

- In 1958 when I was a missionary in what was then
  Northern Rhodesia, the Government decreed that part of
  the Gwembe Valley should be flooded to enlarge Lake
  Kariba. The story goes that the Paramount Chief of the
  tribe in the Valley addressed his people and told them of
  the splendid new houses and gardens awaiting them on
  high ground. The people murmured angrily and would
  not move. A few days later, the Paramount Chief's appeal
  was broadcast from Radio Lusaka. The people heard it
  and moved away without protest. Why? Radio was no
  new thing to them. It was the authority of the disembodied voice. There is danger as well as excitement in
  the power of the disembodied voice: a warning to all
  Christian broadcasters.
  *God-in-a-Box*

## The power of the phone

- In 1949, the *New York Times* reported that Howard
  Unruh, a mad sniper, killed thirteen people then barri-
  caded himself inside his house for a shoot-out to the
  death with the police. Whilst the firing was going on,
  an enterprising reporter discovered the house's phone
  number and rang it. The killer put down his rifle and
  answered the phone. 'What do you want?' he asked. 'I
  can't talk now, I'm busy.'
  *Wrestling with an Angel*

## From weakness to strength

- The Gospel makes its appeal from weakness to strength;
  it is preached from the Cross to the world. The relation-

31

ship of the mass media to the public is the precise opposite. They are immense power-sources. Granted, the viewer or listener has the ultimate sanction in the flick of a switch, but it is one thing to have the ability; quite another to show the will. Hence, in religious broadcasting, there is a jarring incongruity about preaching the Cross using perhaps the most powerful medium of our time.
*God-in-a-Box*

## Far from peripheral

- All forms of mass communication must aim at the central meaning systems of a society, the lives of whose members are mostly governed by simple ideas, broad emotional experiences, predictable tastes and home-spun convictions. Historically, because Western society has been decisively shaped by the Christian religion, its concepts, vocabulary and traditions form one of these central meaning systems. Hence, religion, far from being a peripheral and rather esoteric subject, properly belongs at the heart of mainstream broadcasting.
*Wrestling with an Angel*

## Reality and illusion

- What is reality in the age of the image? A friend who worked in a hospital overheard a visitor saying to a woman with a new-born child, 'What a beautiful baby!' 'That's nothing,' replied the mother proudly. 'You should see her photograph!'
*God-in-a-Box*

## Shaping culture

- There are significant numbers of people in our society who go for weeks without watching a television programme. But they do not go for a day without their lives being shaped by the culture television is creating. Television is doing for human perception what the wheel did for feet. And like the invention of the wheel it marks a decisive turning-point in human history.
  *Cunningham Lecture*

## Global village

- The great communications theorist, Marshall McLuhan, said that television has turned the world into a global village. If so, it is the fake togetherness of a honeycomb of hermits' cells in a cliff wall. The old distinction between private and public spheres of life has become virtually meaningless. These tele-hermits form one huge television audience for a *public* event; they are sharing the same experience, but in *private*, in twos and threes.
  *Cunningham Lecture*

## Life and death reality

- During the Vietnam War, an American pilot bombing Hanoi described the anti-aircraft barrage and fires on the ground as being 'just like a World War Two movie'. Life and death reality was being judged by its approximation to film fantasy. We now live in an *Alice in Wonderland* world where we switch with bewildering frequency between reality and illusion. 'Tweedledee said to Alice, "You won't make yourself a bit realer by crying." Alice replied, "If I wasn't real, I wouldn't be able to cry." "I hope you don't think those are real tears," interrupted Tweedledum crossly.'
  *Hibbert Lecture*

## What is religious broadcasting?

- Religious broadcasting is concerned to answer two questions. First, what is faith doing in the world? And the answer may be anything from worshipping to suffering, with a whole gamut of activities in between. The second question is: what does the world look like through the eyes of faith? These programmes, often documentaries, seek the truth behind the facts, exploring a dimension of depth underlying the passing scene, offering a distinctive perspective on subjects that may also be covered in other areas of broadcasting output such as news or current affairs, science or arts.
  *William Barclay Memorial Lecture*

## Exciting the human spirit

- It was G. K. Chesterton who, in his *Introduction to the Book of Job*, wrote, 'A man can no more possess a private religion than he can possess a private sun and moon.' In a multiverse of private religions, mainstream religious broadcasting, for all its infuriating even-handedness and intellectualism, represents public religion. Its concern is to inform, educate and excite the human spirit. The rest, especially evangelism, is up to the real-life communities of faith – churches, temples, synagogues and mosques.
  *Wrestling with an Angel*

## Bereft of blarney

- The aim of a *Thought for the Day* speaker is to say something witty without being self-consciously clever, serious but not dull, earthed in the real world yet offering the stuff of which dreams are made, religious without being churchy and committed but not dogmatic – rid of rhetoric, purged of purple passages, bereft of blarney.
  *God in the Shower*

## Scylla and Charybdis

- *Thought for the Day* speakers have to navigate between the Scylla of being too pious and the Charybdis of being too political. If they are too fervent, they will be accused of being preachy by the generality of listeners but win approval from churchgoers; if they are undogmatic, they won't upset the agnostic masses but will be written off contemptuously by believers as wishy-washy. And political issues are notoriously difficult to deal with in two minutes thirty seconds. The boundary between a general principle and its party political application is imprecise. It's like one of those frontiers in Africa which you only know you've crossed when someone starts shooting at you.
  *God in the Shower*

## Raw material

- The human spirit-life does not wither because official religion is enfeebled. It still feeds on the raw material of religious experience wherever it may be found. And television is one such source which offers a store of stories, images, models and symbols to keep in trim what could be called the human religious muscles – awaiting a higher manifestation of the Spirit on which they might be exercised.
  *Wrestling with an Angel*

## The starved imagination

- If the religious muscles of secular man and woman are not exercised by traditional religion, they will be brought to bear on this other world of humanly created meaning, television; for we cannot survive without drama, pageant, play and fantasy. When formal religion is privatised and becomes preoccupied with esoteric imagery and

ritual that is inaccessible to the generality of society, a popular piety springs up, searching for other ways of expressing faith. The starved imagination, like the empty belly, is remarkably catholic in its tastes. Writes Gregor Goethals,* 'Until institutional religion can excite the serious play of the soul and evoke the fullness of human passion, television will nurture our illusions of heroism and transcendence.'
*Wrestling with an Angel*

## Theology of the news

- Normality isn't news except in an abnormal situation. A news item that ran, 'Last night there were no shootings or bombings in Little Muddlecome in the Mire' would not rate a mention in a news bulletin, but substitute Beirut, Baghdad or Gaza, and the fact these cities passed a quiet night could well be news. This is to make an important religious assumption about the way the world is intended to be – what believers would call God's good creation; normality. And news is anything recent and interesting which disturbs that state of affairs, the bad news, or reinforces it in striking ways, the good news.
*Hibbert Lecture*

## Meaning and purpose

- It is the news bulletin which drives believers, with par-ticular urgency, to penitence and intercession, because it thrusts at them in stark and up-to-the-minute form the deep questions about meaning, destiny and purpose. That's just a pompous way of saying that the news is the first rough draft of history and the believer has the task of making sense of it.
*Hibbert Lecture*

---

* Gregor Goethals, *The TV Ritual*, Boston, MA, Beacon, 1981, p. 84.

## Shooting the messenger

- It is a venerable tradition to blame communications technology for social disruption. A clear historical line joins the decapitation of bearers of bad news in ancient Greece to the banning of international reporters from Zimbabwe. The invention of printing was held responsible for the upsurge of militant nationalism in fifteenth century Europe and, in the 1930s, the arrival of the first comic books on the scene in America was blamed for rising crime statistics. Now television violence is in the frame. It is possible to show an act of violence on television but not to convey the pain. If scientists ever get round to marketing the 'feelies' of Aldous Huxley's *Brave New World* where television viewers feel the full sensuous impact of what they see, nine-tenths of fictional violence would vanish overnight. Who would want to pay *that* price for realism? The great count against gratuitous television violence is not so much that it desensitises viewers as that it seriously misleads them about the nature of violence in the real world.
*God-in-a-Box*


## Role model

- One reason why television has assumed an undue importance in our culture is that other institutions have declined in significance. For instance, more and more young people depend on television to supply them with models of how other human beings behave in diverse circumstances because most of the alternative sources of role models have shrunk in importance – family, the neighbourhood unit, the community of the work place and, of course, the churches.
*Wrestling with an Angel*

## Theodicy

- Many of the most violent images to be seen on the television screen relate not to any human agency but are the result of natural cataclysm such as earthquake, drought and flood, or of large-scale accidents – acts of God, as we would once have said . . . It is arguable that the main task of the Christian as social commentator confronted with television violence is not so much to demand its removal as to explain its significance. Theodicy is a word not much used these days. It describes that part of theology concerned to defend the goodness and omnipotence of God against objections arising from the existence of evil and suffering in the world. In the television age, this could become the crux of any relevant theology of Christian mission.
*Wrestling with an Angel*

## Shaping society

- No restrictions on television violence, however rigorous, will satisfy the sterner critics. If broadcasters ban Clint Eastwood gunning down his opponents, they will be reviled for allowing Noddy to beat Big Ears over the head with a balloon on a stick. This is not to suggest that public concern is unfounded or can be shrugged off. Broadcasting does its share in shaping society, and if it does not do so by design, it will do it anyway through inadvertence.
*Wrestling with an Angel*

## Pagan vitality

- There is a pagan vitality about television; it generates a life and direction of its own. There is an inherent excitement about the medium that heats the blood of programme producers, so they are tempted to assume that if

the technical problems of making a programme are solved, the value questions will take care of themselves.
*Cunningham Lecture*


## Passing time agreeably

- 'To entertain', so the word means, is to pass time agreeably, and all entertainment is governed by the canons of art – it is the appeal through the senses to the soul, or if that is too problematic a faculty these days, to the mind. And like all art, entertainment is intended to have a tonic or re-creational effect, to replenish rather than to deplete life-energy. The BBC's founder, John Reith, judged a programme by a simple test. He would ask, 'Does this programme say "Yes" to life?' Broadcast entertainment may be assumed to have said 'Yes' to life if at its end people feel better for having heard or seen it. That is no prescription for facile optimism. A drama may lacerate with its realism, but if its lingering impact leaves no room for hope, for the sense that in spite of everything, life still has some point, then it is not true entertainment.
*Drawing the Line*


## Bound for oblivion

- Most programmes are bound for oblivion, and rightly so; the human mind could not contain the torrent of fact, experience and action beamed at it for hours every day. It is one of the strangest graces of creativity that highly talented people are prepared to spend months lavishing skill and care on programmes that will be forgotten moments after the transmission has ended. Entertainment should not be scorned for being ephemeral. These programmes disappear to leave room for experiences which are to be cherished in the memory.
*Drawing the Line*

## Sex and all that

- Sex on the screen usually takes one of three forms: there is the erotic, which is the wholesome celebration of sex as a significant aspect of the human condition. The erotic differs from the obscene in emphasising its joyous and attractive aspects in distinction from its corrupting and disgusting possibilities. There is no moral question mark against it, though as a programme subject care must be taken to avoid scheduling it at times which might risk subjecting children to something for which their learning and life experience have not yet prepared them.
*Drawing the Line*

- The content of pornography is explicit, its immediate intention is to arouse sexual excitement and its ultimate aim is to make money for its producers. Pornography isolates the sex act from its context in human relationships to serve the gratification of appetite. Violence is a key element in much pornography; lust is magnified and distorted by hostility. It is redolent of the hatred and humiliation of women. The moral nihilism it fosters was expressed by the Marquis de Sade who declared, 'I have destroyed everything in my heart that stood in the way of my pleasure.'
*Drawing the Line*

- The third category, the 'obscene', as a matter of word derivation has nothing specifically to do with sex. It is a term of augury meaning 'ill-omened'. What the obscene does is to disgust and offend. Any image which nauseates and repels a reasonably well-adjusted person is obscene even if it has no sexual reference at all – a napalm-burnt child in Vietnam, a grossly mutilated corpse, a scene of egregious gluttony might each be considered obscene, though they would not bring broadcasters into collision with the Obscene Publications bill. The transmission of obscene pictures can occasionally be justified to intro-

duce viewers to new thinking or increase their awareness of the raw nature of the world, but the onus is on the broadcaster to justify any decision to broadcast it; and the fact that a lot of people may watch it is not reason enough.
*Drawing the Line*

- The 625 line grid of television, its structural crudity, favours the obvious and larger than life, images that are shocking over those that are subtle, emphatic emotions rather than gentle ones. The hatreds, rages and turmoils of human character in a flawed world are highly visible; the camera cannot miss them. Wholesome qualities such as love, kindness and goodness do not shout for attention; much of their healing work is done in secret – way beyond the camera's cold eye.
*Drawing the Line*

## A rare virtue

- An important element in wholesome entertainment is reticence. It is a great artistic gift to communicate experience without spelling it out, to coax along the imagination instead of battering it into submission with specific imagery. The true artist knows how to use the allusive, the oblique and the metaphorical to emphasise what is not made obvious. It is not accidental that the converse of reticence, 'explicit', is the word most often used by pornographers to advertise their wares.
*Drawing the Line*

## Freedom of expression

- John Stuart Mill argued for a free market place of ideas where, if all ideas are allowed free expression, good ideas will prevail, and evil ones go to the wall. Sadly I cannot

believe that. In the clash of ideologies, good ideas are often fragile plants which need nurture and protection if they are to survive, and bad ideas have immense vitality in the short run. I do not believe freedom of expression is an isolated virtue. Its exercise must be tempered by the requirements of good order, otherwise the result will be not enlightenment but Bedlam. Liberty is meaningless without limits.
*Ulster University Convocation Lecture*

- Thanks to the revolution centred on the television monitor, the young are seeing history being made before it can be censored by their elders.
  *God-in-a-Box*

## The right to know

- Journalists publishing details of the private lives of the great and the good insist that the public has a right to know. Who gives the public that right? This is to elevate intrusive curiosity into a moral imperative. By virtue of being human, simply that, everyone has the right to an inner sanctum of privacy to which no one has right of access except by invitation. When every shred of privacy is torn aside we are reduced to non-persons. Our God-given identity safeguards the distinction between I and Not-I.
  *'Thought for the Day' – BBC Radio 4*

## Privacy and secrecy

- We often confuse two terms that mean different things, 'privacy' and 'secrecy'. Secrecy is intentional concealment; privacy is deliberate exclusion. Secrecy, as its Latin root suggests, is the hiding of certain knowledge that constitutes power. Privacy is a territorial right, the claim to a personal domain from which the public is excluded. It could be argued that ours is a society in which there is too much secrecy and not enough privacy.

*'Thought for the Day' – BBC Radio 4*

## All things in the light

- The historian Lord Acton wrote, 'Everything secret degenerates. Nothing is safe that cannot bear public scrutiny and discussion.' He could have been echoing Jesus who knew what was in the human heart and would have nothing to do with secret strategies. Again and again he used the metaphors of light and darkness. He said it is of the nature of goodness even when done by stealth to thrust upwards towards the light, whereas evil prefers the safety of darkness where it can flourish in obscurity. He said that there is nothing hidden that will not be revealed, and that his followers should be children of light, everything they do open to public scrutiny as though to the eyes of God.

  *Church and Challenge in a New Africa*

## CAPITALISM

## The Market as God

- It used to be God in whom we lived and moved and had our being; now it is the world Market that has come to dominate our existence as a living power. The economic journalists write about the market as though it has a brain and heart and feelings – they report that the market is 'nervous', or 'unsettled' or 'displeased' or 'cautious' or 'angry'. In fact, they speak of the market the way people used to talk about that other invisible force called God. In Old Testament times, the people feared *Jehovah*'s

reaction to what they'd done. These days, it's the Market's verdict that is awaited with widespread anxiety.
*Things Shaken, Things Unshaken*


## Just how much is enough?

• The Market God is omni-present, it's everywhere, turning the whole of creation into a commodity. You can't escape from it. Bet your life that when astronauts set foot on Mars they'll find a sign advertising Coca-Cola. It now dominates every area of life. For instance, traditional religions have regarded human beings as sacred, but long ago the market reduced them to an inventory of spare parts to be sold a piece at a time – blood, sperm, fertilisable eggs, soon to be added no doubt, human genes. The Market God is insatiable. Its motto is: there is never enough. And this is where the clash of Gods comes in. For one lesson all the great religions teach is that the secret of living in harmony with creation is in knowing just how much *is* enough. How much do we need for the good life? If religion can't face down the market and get that message across, then future generations are going to inherit a bleak world.
*Things Shaken, Things Unshaken*


## The power of self-interest

• In 1776, when John Wesley was preaching a gospel of sacrifice and universal love, Adam Smith, the first of the modern economists, was declaring in *The Wealth of Nations*, 'It is not from the benevolence of the butcher, the brewer or the baker that we expect our dinner, but from regard of their self-interest.' That is an unpalatable truth with which we have to come to terms. The sinews of our life are a tangle of endless contradictions: Governments imprison us in webs of regulations to safeguard our freedom; through taxation, we get stung in order to

enjoy the honey of that hive we call the welfare state, and so on and on. The most illuminating and succinct commentary on this messy and sometimes contradictory state of affairs is to be found in Jesus' parable of the wheat and tares, which allows no room for facile optimism.
*The Hammer of the Lord*


## The Unpoor

- The *Unpoor* have turned greed into the highest form of patriotism. Anything goes as long as it has a favourable effect on the Balance of Payments. The British say, 'If we don't sell arms to X (take your choice amongst poor countries in conflict), someone else will.' Thousands may be robbed of the only thing they have left, life itself, but at least the nice rich will benefit rather than the nasty ones. And it must be some consolation that your child was killed by a bullet made in Britain.
  *Unyoung, Uncoloured, Unpoor*


## Supply and demand

- In his *Rise and Fall of the Third Reich*, William Shirer quotes a business letter that runs: *following our discussion re the delivery of equipment for the burning of bodies, we have pleasure in submitting our plans for redesigned coal ovens which we trust will give satisfaction* . . . There is the ring of the head office about it – oak panelling, lush carpets, svelte secretaries. It is actually talking about a shrieking hell in which mountains of grotesquely stiffened corpses were stacked like logs of wood, the gold fillings in their teeth extracted before being burned. But as they say, that's business. If there is a market for any commodity, it is the capitalist's sacred obligation to supply it.
  *Unyoung, Uncoloured, Unpoor*

### Three-letter word for *Fraud*

- Aid is sometimes a three-letter word meaning fraud. A loan is not aid if the poor country has to sink further into debt to pay it off. Money which must be spent in the donor country on goods which the giver stipulates is not aid but a way of subsidising a rich country's industries. Grants are not Aid but Pieces of Silver if the country which receives them must put up with the bases of foreign troops on her soil or enter into defence pacts. It is not aid but war-mongering to offer a poor country easier payment terms for tanks and military aircraft than for tractors and trucks.
  *Unyoung, Uncoloured, Unpoor*

### Daddy knows best!

- The young are in revolt against the rule of the mandarin, the tribal elder, the wise old man replete with experience who by unchallenged convention sits in the driver's seat. The establishment creed, first foisted on the young in the nursery, 'Daddy knows best!' no longer works. Daddy may know more things but they are the wrong things, or possibly, he knows more things about the wrong world. The young don't see the point of the endless escalator where the eminent elder gets off at the top, clutching his presentation gold watch to allow everyone else to ascend one step nearer the cemetery.
  *Unyoung, Uncoloured, Unpoor*

### Congo chaos

- When the Belgians were forced to grant independence to the Congo, I had a grandstand view of the West's attempts to hang onto the mineral rich Katanga province. Every sordid trick was played – the murder of Patrice Lumumba, the only leader with an outside chance of

uniting the Congo, the inflaming of old tribal hatreds and the employment of white mercenary armies resulted in a devil's stew which finally embroiled the United Nations, Britain, the United States, Russia and China. And in the decades that followed the Congolese have gone on paying the bill with their blood in anarchy, mass murder and territorial incursions. Then the West has the nerve to say, 'That's what happens when you give an African nation independence too soon!'
*Church and Challenge in a New Africa*


## CHANGE

### Thinking out of the box

- In the last resort, there are only two ways of changing things. The first is to think oneself into new ways of acting, the other is to act oneself into new ways of thinking. The first method is rational and analytical, but too often it produces mountains of paper and very little else. The second way is to act in such a way as to change people's thinking. Take the struggle of the Wright brothers to alter people's attitudes towards the possibility of powered flight. These two bicycle makers spent years writing their papers, building models and arguing themselves hoarse. Powered flight by heavier-than-air machines was impossible; that was a mental blockage humans had had for centuries. No less a scientist than the President of the Royal Society had conclusively proved the impossibility of flight in a learned paper. In desperation, Wilbur and Orville Wright put together an outlandish contraption of wood, string and glue. They added a motorcycle engine and one afternoon in 1893 they acted in such a way as to change society's thinking about powered flight for ever. They flew.
*God in the Shower*

## Argument and action

- We spend much time casting around for methods of changing our society which are both moral and effective. Reading a biography of President F. D. Roosevelt I came across this gem of political realism. A pressure group was lobbying him for some reform or other. He listened to the arguments carefully, and then said, 'All right! You've convinced me. Now go out and put pressure on me!' This is a classical example of the relationship between advocacy and action in achieving change. This is what the incarnation is all about – God acting in such a way as to change the world's thinking.
  *Get Through Till Nightfall*

- Very few people are put against a wall and shot just for thinking, provided they keep their thoughts to themselves. Action on the other hand is a form of public communication which can be costly – which is why there is a cross at the heart of Christianity.
  *Get Through Till Nightfall*

## CHURCH

### Put to the test

- Shorn of all the dogma and the supernatural claims made for it, the Church is a community of like-minded believers who commit themselves to an experiment in applied Christianity.
  *The End of the Missionary?*

### The Primacy of the Church

- What we call the gospel is the Church preaching, theology is the Ch-- ' d.inking, worship is the Church addressing

and being addressed by God, the New Testament is the Church remembering, mission is the Church helping God to enlarge the frontiers of the kingdom of heaven, the sacraments are the Church re-enacting the drama of the atonement. You cannot have Jesus without the Church because were it not for the Church we should know virtually nothing about him.
*Bible Reflections Round the Christian Year*


## Beyond our control

- The bursts of Divine power which renew the Church's life are not the result of our strategies but of God's sovereign initiatives. We can say our prayers, plan our programmes, deploy our members, but this totality of our busy-ness is merely kindling, dry faggots which lie inert unless touched by the fire of God. One of the hardest things the Church has to do is to wait. Note those two little words in the New Testament: *not yet*. The author of the Epistle to the Hebrews writes, 'We do *not yet* see all things under subjection to Christ'; Paul cries, 'I have *not yet* reached perfection'; John's Gospel asserts that we are now children of God but it is '*not yet* apparent what we shall be'. The Church's times are in God's hands; we may mould the passive clay, but only the Spirit can breathe life into it; we may arrange the skeleton, but only the Spirit can command, 'Oh ye dry bones, live!'
  *Whit Sunday sermon – Liverpool Cathedral*

- Christians can be divided roughly into two groups, mystics and militants – those who know and those who burn.
  *Snapshots*

- If the traditionalist tends to take refuge in piety to avoid the claims of action, the liberal is tempted to take refuge in action from the claims of piety.
  *The Hammer of the Lord*

49

## One company

- However we gather and from whence we come, slowly
  but surely we cease to be a random assembly, an *ad hoc*
  crowd and become part of God's earthly history. We are
  of that same company who followed Moses into the
  desert, who wept in exile by the waters of Babylon, who
  claimed to follow Jesus but failed to do what he commanded, who heard with disbelief of the empty tomb,
  who saw the Spirit at Pentecost sting all present with
  tongues of living flame, who have lived through the glory
  and humiliation of the historical church. We affirm the
  God of Abraham, Isaac and Jacob, of Wesley – what God
  was to them, he will be to us and those who come after
  us.
  *Sermon at Re-opening of Wesley's Chapel, 1978*

## A mystery and a mess

- Take a few names at random – Billy Graham and
  Reinhold Niebuhr, Albert Schweitzer and Martin Luther
  King, William Temple and Dick Sheppard, Mother
  Teresa and Pope John Paul II, Cliff Richard and John
  Tavener – any Church that can contain them all is both a
  mystery and a mess – a great, sprawling, untidy organism
  whose centre is fixed but whose circumference is impos-
  sible to define. And that's how it should be, for only
  Christ knows his own.
  *The Hammer of the Lord*

## Bread for that day only

- There is an illegitimate kind of appeal to the authority of
  the Church as guardian of a deposit of indisputable
  divine truth. But as the people of Israel learned, if you try
  to hoard manna it goes bad. In the Lord's Prayer, Jesus

warned us that we are only given our bread for that day. Faith exists as a continuous inner warfare; we have to win it afresh constantly. Each morning the Christian confronts God's world in all its horror and glory and asks, 'In the face of all this, do I still believe?'
*'Neglected Themes in Modern Preaching'*

## Ecclesiastical inertia

• In spite of all its attempts at reform and retrenchment, the Church cannot be changed beyond recognition because any institution which has survived for two thousand years has accumulated a massive degree of inertia, in the strict sense of that term – the tendency of a body to continue on the same path unless disrupted by a considerable force. The Church is inevitably conservative because it must continually refer to the remote past in order to refresh its memory about the reasons for its existence. The early Fathers talked about the 'church from Abel on' – which is going back a very long way.
*Bugles in the Afternoon*

## More like Mother

• The conservatism of the Church does not prevent it from throwing up radical movements from time to time. Reformers such as Luther, Wesley and William Booth may have struck out in new directions but they were still the children of the old Church and never disavowed it even when it disowned them. To the end of his life, Luther described the Church that excommunicated him as his 'Holy Mother' and John Wesley insisted he would live and die a loyal son of the Church of England. In time, all splinter movements tend to lose their initial momentum and settle down into a sedate middle age where the older they get the more they begin to resemble their

mother, and so fall under the same laws of growth and decay.
*Methodist Recorder*


## By whose side

- Though I would like to call myself a rebel, I cannot cut myself free from the Church. This is not only because I have a personal share of responsibility for her failures and so must stand the racket, but also because it is through the cracked and distorting mirror of the Church that I first saw the One by whose side I seek to take my stand in the life of the world.
  *Include Me Out!*


## Mind-forged manacles

- It's as though the communion table were a great anvil to which we come in order to have what William Blake called 'mind-forged manacles' smashed off, for the Gospel is a hammer which shatters the constricting images that imprison us like a plaster cast. We can be free both of the images others impose on us and those we impose on ourselves. The only image that matters is the image God has of us.
  *Let God be God*


## The cult of bigness

- Even in its weakened state, the Church may still be too big rather than too small to be an effective instrument of God's will. Jesus never founded a mass movement and showed no interest in building larger and stronger churches. His constant preoccupation was with the Kingly rule of God, whose working unit is two or three

gathered in his name. His parables teach that it is by small scale operations the Kingdom spreads, seed growing secretly underground or yeast fermenting imperceptibly in a lump of dough.
*Methodist Recorder*

## Lacking punch

- Perhaps as a church we fall short of our calling not because our zeal is fitful but because too much of our thinking is superficial. To use the Pauline analogy of the Body – our muscles are well-exercised, it is our brain cells that are under-nourished. Our attack lacks punch because our main armament is not the Spirit's sword which cuts to the heart of great issues, but the jester's balloon on a stick which pats them fondly on the head.
*The Hammer of the Lord*

## Picture of redemption

- The Church is a laboratory of the Kingdom in which the promises of God are put to the test of practicability. It is meant to present society with a living picture of what redemption could mean for it.
*Church and Challenge in a New Africa*

## Communion of love

- Like all sacraments, the Church is grace made visible, and visibility implies some structure – the church and not-the-church must be distinguishable. But because it is *grace* that is made visible, the emphasis is on a communion of love rather than a legally constituted body.
*God-in-a-Box*

## Liberation

- When the Republic of Zambia became independent at midnight on October 23rd, 1964, thousands of people gathered together in the streets and on hill tops to wait out the hours of darkness. Then as the sun rose on the first day of their liberation, the birth of nationhood, they danced and wept crying, 'We're free!' And by God, so are we free! Beneath all our solemn ceremonial, there ought always to be the same immoderate joy threatening to break surface and upset the measured tread of our liturgies. For if the Church does not meet as forgiven sinners reliving the miracle of their liberation, then the Church does not meet at all.
*Out of Africa's Crucible*

## God's secret

- The true state of the Church is a secret known only to God; its members are the worst judges of its health or sickness. We cannot assess the Church's condition by the size of its membership, its financial balance sheet or the condition of its buildings. There have been periods when the Church was aglow with secular power and influence, but beneath her splendid outward aspect her heart was shrivelled and almost dead. At other times, the Church has been laid waste, her priests dead or in hiding, her buildings in ruins, and yet in upper rooms and cellars, believers gathered in secret to pore over the Bible, break bread together and proclaim in a whisper the Lord's death until he comes. A great new age was about to dawn.
*Methodist Recorder*

- The besetting sin of the radical is to offer redemption to a world that is not interested in it whilst denying it to the Church which, for all its faults, prays for it constantly.
*Include Me Out!*

## A way out of the tomb

- A few years ago I returned to Africa to make a docu-
mentary for BBC Radio 4 in which I relived the experiences of thirty years earlier. On this return trip I went to a
remote village in the Zambezi Valley where one of my old
missionary friends had worked for years. When he came
back to Britain, the Methodist Church did not replace him
because the work had died out. He had only three con-
verts to show for his time there. One died, another became
an evangelist and moved away and a third reverted to the
old religion. But when I went back I found there at the
heart of the village not a ruin but a neat, thatched-roof,
burnt-brick church from which came the sounds of a
choir practising for the following Sunday's services. There
can only be one explanation. The Church has a Lord who
can find his way out of a tomb.
*Glory Days – BBC Radio 4*


## Jesus without Christianity

- There are Christian radicals whose eagerness to see the
Church virtually wiped out is almost pathological. Every
sign of decline is evidence of approaching victory. Losses
in membership demonstrate that the Church is doing its
job. They relish Jesus' words, 'I came not to bring peace
but a sword,' and believe the blade should first be thrust
at the Church's throat, cutting away the decaying flesh
accumulated over two thousand years. They burn to get
back to Jesus and make a fresh start; they want Jesus
without Christianity and Christianity without the
Church. They would take as their motto the final words
of Professor Herbert Butterfield's 1950s BBC Reith
Lectures, 'Hold to Christ, and for the rest be totally
uncommitted.' But with all respect to the great historian,
that just isn't possible. We cannot distil out the spiritual
essence of Christianity, 100% proof, from its flesh and

blood, brick and mortar incarnations in churches. The People of the Way have accumulated much luggage on their march through history. They cannot disavow either the glory or the misery of their past.
*Methodist Recorder*

## Who is to blame?

• Traditional Christians may be resistant to radical change but they are rarely complacent. They are very conscious of their failures in faith and discipleship, yet an unbiased observer might conclude that the Church has been the victim rather than the villain in the story of the volcanic decades since the Second World War. It is hard to see how the present state of the churches is *primarily* the result of anything believers have done or are failing to do. Faithful churchgoers continue to put ever more urgency into their prayer and witness as they see the pews empty. And ceaselessly, they beseech God for a religious revival like those that have swept church and nation from time to time in past centuries. The one conclusion they find hard to accept is that God might be saying 'No' to denominational revival.
*The Christian Conundrum – BBC Radio 2*

## Not Siamese twins

• Just as Christ walked on water, so there have been times when the Christian faith seems to have walked on air as the Church collapsed under it. This apparent defiance of the law of gravity is possible because at such times the reality of the faith has been embodied in the secretly present kingdom. It is a grave error to assume that the Church and the Kingdom are inextricably joined together like Siamese twins – if one is sick, the other must be ailing.
*Things Shaken, Things Unshaken*

## Enthusiasm

- We humans are strange creatures; there are some people who would be prepared to be burned but not bored for Christ's sake; who can't spare half an hour of their time in their busy schedules yet might give their whole lives to a cause if their imaginations are fired. The Greek origin of the word 'enthusiasm' is *entheos*, inspired by a god. We need more of that.
*Methodist Recorder*

## Mankind my Church

- I think it was Gordon Rupp who pointed out that there is a Cinderella-like quality about the Church. There she is at the world's service, up to her elbows in muck, to be found grubby and tattered amongst the pots and pans. Only to the eye of faith can it be seen that beneath the rags she is adorned like a bride for her husband.
*Bible Reflections Round the Christian Year*

## In its entirety

- Where the Church exists at all, it exists in its entirety. If the one, holy, catholic and apostolic Church is not to be found wherever half a dozen Christians gather, it is not to be found at all. To them fall all its duties and responsibilities; all its privileges and blessings are theirs.
*Bible Reflections Round the Christian Year*

- Truly there are a thousand things wrong with the Church but, for all its faults, it is the only guardian of a Gospel without which humanity is lost.
*Out of Africa's Crucible*

## The pure and the responsible

- The American poet Archibald Macleish said there are only two kinds of people, the pure and the responsible. In that division the Church always stands amongst the responsible rather than the pure; the engaged rather than the detached; amongst the red-blooded reckless rather than the anaemically dignified. And this, because we follow Jesus who plunged into a Jordan soiled by a thousand bodies, lived amongst publicans and sinners, died alongside criminals and rose again out of a cemetery of decaying corpses.
*Mankind My Church*

## CHURCH UNION

## When God says No

- No historical movement, not even one associated with the name of Wesley, has an unconditional right of indefinite existence. 'The grass withers, the flower fades, surely the people is grass,' warned Isaiah, and added that it is the word of God which endures; but, as Paul reminds us, the treasure is contained in perishable clay vessels. Perhaps this clay vessel we call our particular church is coming to the end of its useful life. That is not defeatism but an acknowledgement of God's sovereignty. The God who, according to Jesus, is able to raise up stones as sons of Abraham is never without fresh initiatives, new ways of accomplishing his purposes. Perhaps he has other plans for us.
*Methodist Recorder*

- The underlying motive for some proposals for closer union between churches in decline is sheer survival: like the Irishman who said, 'You add your debts to mine and

we'll be twice as rich!' It's like mooring a sinking ship to
one that won't float.
*Methodist Recorder*


## Spiritual hybrids

• Only churches secure in their traditions and confident of
their place in the universal Church are ready to pursue
further unions. Any union between mealy-mouthed
Methodists, apathetic Anglicans, careless Catholics and
pallid Presbyterians could only add a breed of spiritual
hybrids so accommodating they would add the Devil to
the Trinity to avoid offending their friendly neighbourhood Satanists.
*Presidential Address – 1976*


## Denominational decline

• There is little appetite amongst modern believers for
restoring the confessional boundaries of the past. Increasingly, it is spiritual emphases which draw Christians
together or keep them apart. Charismatics in the Church
of England feel more at home alongside their Methodist
counterparts than among fellow-Anglicans who hold to a
different tradition. The evangelical alliances welcome all-
comers who share similar attitudes to biblical authority
and a common vocabulary for expressing their loyalty
to Jesus; they show little interest in denominational
allegiances. These days, most enquirers don't worry overmuch about the name displayed on the notice board outside the church.
*The Christian Conundrum – BBC Radio 2*

• Consumerism has eaten into the very soul of our society
as people shop around for their spiritual as well as
physical needs. The world is no more sold on a single

59

Church than it would be on a single TV channel, super-store or political party.
*The Christian Conundrum* –*BBC Radio* 2

## Evolution versus Resurrection

- My problem with the traditional doctrine of Apostolic Succession is that it is a clear case of elevating Evolution over Resurrection, and trusting in dead ancestors rather than a living Christ.
  *Bugles in the Afternoon*

## Legitimate differences

- I have never really understood what is meant by the 'sin' of disunity. Certainly, backbiting, exclusiveness and factionalism are sins, but they are much more likely to be found within rather than between denominations. The glory of being human is that we enjoy a wide diversity of tastes, aptitudes and perceptions about everything under the sun; yet apparently, if our apprehension of God is not uniform we are in error. It may be a waste of resources or even a tragedy that there is not one universal church, but how can it be sinful? Inherent differences are facts of life not evidences of moral failure.
  *Methodist Recorder*

## Realities that defy definition

- Christians within the mainstream churches are finding unity within, beyond and in spite of existing structures, if you like, bottom-up ecumenicity – they are just getting on with it and like Nelson turning a blind eye to the theological niceties. We are moving into uncharted spirit-ual territory, wrestling with realities that defy definition rather than being stuck with definitions devoid of reality.
  *Methodist Recorder*

## Meccano-model union

- Top-down Church union schemes are a product of a twentieth century corporate culture where institutions merge by way of negotiation and compromise, horse-trading and take-over. This is the Meccano-model theory of church unity and runs: if we can bolt together the Anglicans and Methodists in this generation and then join the resulting structure to the Catholics in the next, and so on and on, eventually all the pieces will unite to create a super-Church. But Christianity is diversifying faster than the mainstream Churches can heal their breaches.
*Methodist Recorder*

## A rich complexity

- Achieving merger amongst Christians is like trying to get the dent out of a ping-pong ball, you smooth it out in one place and a declivity appears somewhere else. This is the way Christianity is and always has been, a many-splendoured thing, reflecting the rich complexity of the human nature Christ took upon himself.
*Include Me Out!*

## Flat earth theology

- Put starkly: is the Methodist tradition exhausted or has it the capacity to renew itself? And if so, can this be done in isolation from the Church of England which was the source of its original inspiration? There are good reasons for union with the Church of England, provided it is free of Establishment. It would make no more sense for Methodism to become part of an *established* church at the beginning of the 21st century than it would to revert to a belief that the earth is flat.
*Bugles in the Afternoon*

## The Nonconformist principle

• Methodism became a Church by accident, against the wishes of its earthly founder, so I am prepared to see it like leaven swallowed up in a larger lump. The one thing I would fight to retain is the Nonconformist principle, by which I do not mean some regrouping of the Free Churches but a renewed emphasis on the centrality of prophetic as opposed to priestly religion. This is a tension that goes way back beyond the Reformation into the Old Testament and the squabbles between Moses and Aaron. I do not deny the validity or importance of priestly religion, Christianity could not have survived without it, but the wholeness of the Gospel requires that the healthy tension between priestly and prophetic strains in our faith should be maintained. If either were to be swallowed by the other, the result would be a partial and deformed representation of Christ.
*Methodist Recorder*

## Which Golden Age?

• I can't see any New Testament ground for arguing that in itself a big church has more value than two small ones, just as a pound coin has no more value than two fifty pence pieces. After all, Methodist Union in 1932 created one church from three but did not stem the decline; the United Reformed Church is a union church but it has continued to shrink since the Congregationalists and Presbyterians came together. It has always seemed to me from my limited reading of church history that this desire of church union enthusiasts to recreate an apostolic Golden Age when Christianity was pure and undefined, when there was one Church and, except for the odd heretic, all Christians were one in faith and hope and charity is a myth. Was there ever an original Golden Age when the Church was whole and the faith pure and

uncontested? Indeed, the New Testament talks much more often about churches than the Church.
*Mankind My Church*


## COMMUNICATION

### Divine gossip

- Ours is a talkative God. Genesis tells us that God talked the universe into existence. Nowhere is there any suggestion that God did *anything*; he spoke and the universe appeared – 'and God said, "Let there be light!" and there was light'. Lawyers talk of 'uttering' a document; God uttered the universe. According to Isaiah, the very universe was made from the breath God expelled when he spoke. And one of the most extraordinary verses in Scripture occurs in the Book of Exodus: 'The Lord used to speak to Moses face to face as a man speaks with his friend.'
  *God-in-a-Box*


### Wrestling with an angel

- There is a story in Genesis of Jacob wrestling with an unknown adversary by the River Jabbok. According to different traditions, Jacob was struggling either against an angel or God himself. It is a picture of divine–human communication. Jacob is not quite sure who his adversary is, which points to the ambiguity of all communication with God; it can only be a matter of faith, not certainty. Jacob is injured in the struggle, which hints at the cost of such communication. And it is a wrestling match not a Socratic dialogue; they collided in close encounter. Getting to grips with God is a daunting task.
  *God-in-a-Box*

## Self-disclosure

- Communication is about the encounter between personalities who, whatever they gain by way of knowledge in the process, discover more about the other and themselves as a result. That is the crucial distinction between two terms we tend to use interchangeably – *information* and *communication*. To *inform* is to exchange bits of intelligence; to *communicate* is to disclose something of oneself in the act of passing on the bits of intelligence. I remember standing in the concourse of a railway station during a signalmen's strike. Over the loudspeaker there had issued a constant stream of messages about delays and cancellations, but this time, the announcer suddenly said, 'You've no idea how embarrassed I feel at having to keep telling you all this!' Everyone on the station froze and looked up, startled. That announcer had been informing us, but she began to communicate with us when she revealed her feelings.
  *Agnellus Andrew Memorial Lecture*


## Partial unveiling of God's nature

- The Christian contention is that what is passed on from God to human beings is not just knowledge, however profound, but life, and not just life but divine life through Jesus Christ. The crux of Christian communication is nothing less than a partial unveiling of God's nature, for according to the New Testament, Christ is the communicated self-expression of God.
  *Wrestling with an Angel*

## One and only way

- It is the primary purpose of theology to offer solutions to specific problems which might hinder God's self-disclosure. Thus, in one sense, the theology of communication is the only sort of theology there is.
  *Wrestling with an Angel*

## The go-between God

- Any system of communication requires a network with some degree of permanence. The Christian grid is called the communion of the Holy Spirit. In Bishop John V. Taylor's phrase, the gap between God and believers is bridged by the go-between God. The Holy Spirit provides the energy that enables Christians to be fully present to one another in self-disclosure.
  *Wrestling with an Angel*

## Mechanisation of the message

- Is it an utterly outrageous thought that something quite fundamental went out of Christianity the first time an early apostle need no longer look an enquirer in the eye and tell him about Jesus but could instead say, 'This is a Gospel. Read it'; or in the twenty-first century, a believer might say, 'Listen to this broadcast or watch this television programme!'? Possibly at that point a link in the chain of apostolic succession snapped. The mechanisation of the message by whatever means – writing, print, electronic media – is speech without speaker, image without presence, contact without personal engagement. Every form of Christian communication other than face-to-face encounter is in some way defective.
  *Agnellus Andrew Memorial Lecture*

## Dynamic discourse

- God's revelation is not confined to words – it can be an event whose nature exposes something about the meaning of all events, a happening in history that sums up what history is about. The Christian revelation was specific, it was done 'under Pontius Pilate', yet it is universal in expressing all that God has done and intends to do with his world. It is local because it happened in Palestine and yet is transcendent because its origins and destiny are beyond history; and it is dynamic – it mediates power as well as offering explanation.
*Bible Reflections Round the Christian Year*


## From communication to communion

- When the communications gap between God and his creatures has not just been bridged but transcended, communication solidifies into communion. There is unity not just of meaning but of life. The Bible is silent about the detail of the unimaginable condition when God had disclosed as much about himself as his creatures can bear. It is a state described by terms such as *kabod* in the Old Testament and *doxa* in the New Testament. Glory.
*God-in-a-Box*


## No more messages

- In the old days, God communicated to his people by sending messages through his prophets and seers. Then, according to the Christian account of things, he decided to stop sending messages and come himself, meeting us face to face. As Job put it, 'I had heard of thee by the hearing of mine ear but now mine eye seeth thee.' In Jesus, message and messenger become one.
*God in the Shower*

## Story telling

- The early Church was a community of story tellers. They got that habit from the Old Testament which had little to say about philosophical notions, and instead told stories about miraculous beginnings, floods, burning bushes, sacred mountains, exoduses and exiles. The first Christians endlessly told a story about victory over death. Whilst their scholars attacked polytheism and made use of the ideas of contemporary philosophy such as the *logos* to build a cultural bridge to intellectual non-believers, the disciples went on telling the same story to their children, to casual contacts and all they met in the street. Sailors carried the tale off to distant ports; slaves told their masters. The Gospel was brief, urgent in tone and free from the overblown rhetoric of pagan orators. And it was a story that could be easily memorised.
  *Wrestling with an Angel*


## CONVERSION

## Wholeness

- The New Testament was not intended to be a pre-programmed compendium of answers to every conceivable problem the human condition can throw up. The notion that Christianity ought to have something to say about everything is one of the fashionable heresies of our time. In fact, the whole New Testament is massively concentrated on one question; how may I and my world be made whole? The Biblical word is 'salvation', but it means the same thing. And the traditional term for the process by which this quest for wholeness begins is conversion.
  *Sermon – Wesley's Chapel*

## Pressure points

- The acid test of conversion is not just the effect it has on a person's prayer life or Bible-reading, you'd expect it to change them. But, what change has it made at the pressure points of our lives? And the pressure points of our lives have to do with our attitudes to money, sex, ambition, power, justice, race and the like. If conversion does not affect them, then it is not conversion as the New Testament understands it.
*Sermon – Wesley's Chapel*

## Strategy to renew the world

- Far from being world-denying and pietistic, Christian conversion is a central element in any strategy to renew the world. Because we have been justified by God we must engage in the struggle for social and political justice; because we have been reconciled to God, we must seek reconciliation in all human relationships; because we have made our peace with God, we can become still centres of the crusade for worldly peace; and because we know the joy of salvation we can add to the store of this world's gaiety.
*Starting from Scratch*

## Eye to Eye

- Conversion means being able to look someone in the eye and recognise that they are sharers with us in the death and resurrection of Jesus, and feel a bond that ties us together more closely than any physical or cultural or racial relationship could.
*William Barclay Memorial Lecture*

## An instinct for reality

- Plato defined religion as an instinct for reality. Jesus came to save the world and he is able to save men and women from anything – except illusion. Recall that phrase in the story of the Prodigal Son – '*And when he came to himself*, he went to his father.' So long as he lived in a half world of delusion, no one could do anything for him. Only when he returned to the real world did he come within the range of salvation. Jesus was incarnate in the real world, died and rose again here and that is where his Spirit operates. There can be no salvation from a world that doesn't exist. People must come to terms with the reality of their plight before they can be healed.
  *Starting from Scratch*

## On packing a suitcase

- When sceptics say religion is irrelevant to the business of every day living, they're saying in effect that everything is important with the exception of, well, everything. We can't exclude religion from our thinking because it's the very frame round our thinking. It would be like packing a suitcase and leaving out the case. Whether we like it or not we have a general view of existence which colours everything we say and do. And that's our religion.
  *Starting from Scratch*

## Before winter

- The uncertainty of life injects urgency into our dealings with God as with all else. David said to Jonathan, 'There is but one step between me and death.' There is only one step between any of us and death. An old rabbi was asked by one of his disciples when he ought to make his peace with God. The rabbi thought for a moment and then said, 'Oh, not until one minute before you die.' 'But,

Master,' protested the disciple, 'I don't know when I shall die.' 'Exactly,' said the rabbi. 'Do it now.'
*Mankind My Church*

## Act like a believer

- Sometimes the only proof that something is so reveals itself after we have acted. Jesus recommended this principle as a jumping off point for faith. The first demand he made on his followers wasn't that they should think beautiful thoughts about him but that they should follow him: 'Do what I command,' he said. Act like a believer. To act as if God exists is to pray as if there is someone who hears our prayers. It is to love our neighbour as if God commanded it. That is how G. K. Chesterton became a Christian. Though prayer meant nothing to him personally, he took it up as a discipline because it meant a lot to godly people whom he admired. He hoped that by living as if prayer worked he might get the point. And he did.
*Start Your Own Religion*

- Though God made us without our consent, he cannot redeem us without it.
*A Week in the Life of God*

## COURAGE

### Moral consistency

- As a quality, courage is closely allied to constancy or integrity. We must have the constancy to live invariably by the moral values we prize – yesterday, today and tomorrow; in all possible circumstances, applying them indiscriminately to our roles in life as fathers, mothers,

husbands, wives, neighbours and citizens; otherwise they are not virtues but tactics. It is courage which guarantees consistency in moral behaviour. Without courage, all other virtues are impotent; without courage, personal life is not worth the candle.
*Starting from Scratch*

## Rusting equipment

- There is no worthwhile human activity that does not involve an element of risk, physical, emotional or moral. For human potential to blossom we need a cause greater than ourselves; one that will not exhaust itself before we exhaust ourselves. There are none so sad as those who have outlived the causes for which they risked all. They linger like the rusting equipment of some long aban- doned experiment, awaiting a ghostly command to start up again that never comes.
*Starting from Scratch*

## Cowardice?

- I recall my father who served in the trenches in the First World War talking about one of his comrades who had served with him through the great set-piece battles, Loos, the Somme, Ypres. One day they were throwing the bodies of dead Germans into a huge shell crater to be rid of the sight and smell of them. This man suddenly stood up and said, 'Enough! This butchery is madness!' 'He was', said my father, 'the bravest of us all. When the officer's whistle blew and we went over the top again, he stayed behind in the trench. In No Man's Land we had an even chance of survival, but when he disobeyed that order, he was a dead man.'
*God in the Shower*

## Virtue at the limit

- We describe courage as a virtue, but there's a sense in which it is just any of the other virtues lived out persistently – so it is love or truth or goodness and so on carried through to the end.
  *Get Through Till Nightfall*

## Hazardous faith

- Every significant human activity involves courage because we are reaching towards some goal which is not within our grasp and may never be. The risk may be physical, emotional or moral as we put ourselves within range of danger. No faith is beyond challenge, no belief so credible it is immune from attack, no conviction exempt from jeopardy. Much of faith's value depends on the element of hazard in it.
  *Start Your Own Religion*

## CREEDS

## Precise fit

- A creed is like a key which has a precise shape and will only work if its distinctive notches and gaps remain absolutely fixed. Let one be worn down by a fraction of an inch and the key will not open the lock. This is why the early Christians battled for generations over the odd syllable of a Greek theological term. The word in contention was tiny but the issue was a matter of life and death to them; it determined their view of the universe.
  *Start Your Own Religion*

## The dimensions of God

- Our inability to fill the God-shaped blank in our society with idols outlines the true dimensions of God as dramatically as the statements about him in the creeds.
*Methodist Recorder*


## Credal Oneness

- The Creed says the Church is One, Apostolic and Holy, but its early history shows how hard it was to be all three at once. The nearer the Church got to its boasted Oneness by trying to build a unified power base in Rome or Constantinople, the less Holy and Apostolic it became. The wider its imperial writ ran, the shallower its penetration, the higher its secular ambitions, the more worldly its spirit.
*Methodist Recorder*


## Paper pilgrimage

- The creeds summarise the beliefs of an abstraction; what Scotland Yard would call Identikit Man or Woman. Not even the wisest or godliest of Church fathers or theologians can predict precisely what form faith will take when the Spirit possesses a unique human personality. The creeds bear as much or as little resemblance to anyone's real-life faith as a railway timetable does to an actual journey. *Bradshaw's Guide* sets out in neat lists of towns and times the standard journey from say, London to Manchester. But that is a paper pilgrimage. It takes no account of the possibility that the train might be held up at Watford or be forced to make a detour around Wilmslow. Of course, in the travel business there are agents who will map out our route and detail our connection, and all we have to do is to follow their instructions. But in the world of faith we cannot act through

agents and pay people to discover God on our behalf, not even if they wear clerical collars or occupy university chairs of theology. Everybody must make his or her own estimate of the meaning and point of life, and then turn it into a truth to live by. And that exploration into God, that journey and experience, is our own path, however much the sheepdogs of official religion snap at our heels and try to drive us along predetermined routes.
*God in a Shower*

- Without a creed, believers wouldn't know which God to call on. Indeed, without a creed how do I know that the person sitting next to me in the pew worships the same God?
*Start Your Own Religion*


## DEMOCRACY

### No biblical sanction

- However much Western Christians sing the praises of democracy as the best form of government, it is important to remember that the Bible does not baptise any particular kind of state. As the Old Testament records, the people of Israel in their long journey through history flourished or suffered under many political systems – theocracy (Judges 8), absolute monarchy (1 Samuel 24), anarchy (Judges 21), Princeship (Ezekiel 40), slavery (Babylonian captivity), priest-kingship (Maccabees) and imperialism (Rome). The Bible's only interest in any form of government seems to have been whether it was the agent of God's righteousness or the rod of his anger.
*Things Shaken, Things Unshaken*

## Whose Voice?

- Archbishop Reynolds was tragically wrong and thoroughly unbiblical when he declared at the coronation of Edward III, 'The Voice of the people is the Voice of God!' It is obvious that the Voice of the people can be the Voice of the very Devil when they cry, 'Give us Barabbas!' or *'Seig Heil!'*
  *'Thought for the Day'* – *BBC Radio 4*

## From parish hall to Downing Street

- Democracy's strength is that it can constantly renew itself because it harnesses the skills and gifts of anyone at any level in society. There are mini-democracies to be found in the church, golf club, trade union branch, women's institute and dozens of community societies. Here its techniques are practised – debating and voting on policy issues, keeping proper accounts and accurate minutes, electing officers, canvassing people, accepting the verdict of the majority. It is part of the genius of democracy that a man or woman can start out by chairing the local pigeon fanciers' society and end up presiding at a cabinet meeting in No. 10 Downing Street.
  *Church and Challenge in a New Africa*

## Choices! Choices!

- We say democracy is about giving the people free choice, but choice is meaningless unless there are different things to choose from. Statesmanship means sometimes sharpening the options rather than allowing them to blur into a dirty mishmash of moderation we miscall political harmony.
  *Unyoung, Uncoloured, Unpoor*

### Testifies to the truth

- By making room for personal reconciliation amongst those who are political opponents, democracy not only preserves the peace and good order of the community but testifies to the truth that there is a realm even more important than politics where humanity is being reconciled to God by the power of Christ.
  *Things Shaken, Things Unshaken*

## ENVIRONMENT

### Mother Earth

- If God is our father, the earth is our mother. We didn't come into this world, we came out of it, and if we don't stop our polluting and poisoning it, future generations yet unborn won't be.
  *'Thought for the Day'* – *BBC Radio 4*

### A holy place

- That huge jolly mystic G. K. Chesterton confessed he never ceased to be amazed at the wetness of water, the fierceness of fire, the steeliness of steel and the muddiness of mud. The knack of living creatively is both to be at home in the world and constantly astonished at it. By virtue of being human we are a chosen people, whoever we are, and we live in a holy place, wherever it is, because we have inherited God's creation.
  *Start Your Own Religion*

- Remember the good old days when only God could end the world? Now we can end it, but can we save it, or have we become our own doomsday machine?
  *'Thought for the Day'* – *BBC Radio 4*

## Personal story

- I may be nothing much in the great scheme of things, but I am the product of an amazingly complex cosmic process. If God indeed made me, he had to create most of the rest of the universe to do it; the scholars say that life emerged from the sea as a dot of tissue – oceans and atmospheres and tides and sun and moon conspired to throw up the life-bearing blob that became me. My auto-biography begins with a bang called Creation.
  *Starting from Scratch*


## Cash machine computing

- The other day I went to use a cash machine and found that some of its functions weren't working; it would let me have money, but it couldn't tell me what the remaining balance of my account was. So I found myself withdrawing less than I otherwise might have done, just to be on the safe side, because I didn't know how much was still left. That's the way it is with the earth. We have a global life account, being born on a planet with finite resources; when they've gone, they've gone. We might be able to compute roughly how much of our life account we have spent, but we don't really know how much is left. So is it not suicidal irresponsibility to squander the heritage of future generations?
  *'Thought for the Day'* – *BBC Radio 4*

- If my neighbour might be defined as anyone whose actions could affect me, who, then, in the entire wide world, is not my neighbour?
  *Starting from Scratch*

## Genesis in reverse

• The way we are treating the planet, it may soon be necessary to record not how things began but how they will end – a sort of Genesis in reverse. It might run something like this. In the end, though humankind had nowhere else to go, they systematically demolished the home God had given them. They plundered the earth and slaughtered their brothers and sisters of the animal kingdom. And this was the seventh day from the end.

They polluted the crystal clear air with the fumes of their machines and poisoned the sea with garbage and turned rivers into foaming torrents of chemical waste and began ever so slowly to choke themselves to death. And this was the sixth day from the end.

And though God created humanity to be one, they divided out those who thought and prayed as they did from those who thought and prayed differently, the former they called allies and the latter enemies, and they began to fear those they had cut themselves off from. And this was the fifth day from the end.

And they said the strong are entitled to most of what's going and the weak can have the rest. But the more they had to lose, the greater became their fear of those who had nothing to lose, so they built ever higher walls and larger armies to protect their self-interest. And they were deaf to the voice of the poor whose pleas were turning into a terrible anger. And this was the fourth day from the end.

And they slept uneasily and awoke afraid and set to work to create the ultimate weapon. Then they said, 'Now we feel safe.' But their enemies didn't feel safe and so they too created an ultimate weapon, and the whole earth lived nervously under the shadow of extinction and called it peace. And this was the third day from the end.

Then having proved by technical skill that they could make anything, they said, 'Now, let us make God in our own image: let us gaze into a mirror and worship the one we see there.' And this was the second day from the end.

And they gazed in rapture upon the gleaming products of their own ingenuity and cried, 'Bigger! Faster! Stronger! Richer! Louder! More!' And they became frantic with a desire nothing could satisfy. And that was the day before the end.

And at the end there was chaos and uproar, and when the din subsided human life had vanished. And the ravished earth rested on the seventh day.

Then God spoke. 'Back to the drawing board,' he said sadly.

*'Thought for the Day' – BBC Radio 4*

## ETERNAL LIFE

### God is not an accessory

- In any discussion about the afterlife, we must begin not with any questions to do with our personal survival, our human hopes and desires, but with God and God alone. Our very preoccupation with the afterlife can blind us to the truth that we are not the centre of the universe; Creation's main purpose is not to guarantee our personal survival, with God an accessory to the process.
  *'Neglected Themes in Modern Preaching'*

### Heaven's above

- There is God's creation and there is God; they are the only two realities. Traditionally we have believed in the metaphor of heaven as a spiritual realm above and beyond this one, a place or condition of higher existence over which God presides, surrounded by the heavenly host. In fact, Jesus sometimes uses the term 'heaven' as

another word for God; as for example, in 'Was the baptism of John from heaven or from man?' or the prodigal son confessing, 'I have sinned against heaven.' Therefore, to be in heaven is to be in God.
*'Neglected Themes in Modern Preaching'*


## Remembered by God

• 'And God remembered . . .' is an expression commonly found in the Bible drawing attention to God's continuing care for those whom he calls to mind. Unlike ours, God's memory is not in the past, because he has no past: God is the eternal Now. Our historical existence had a beginning and it will have an end, but it is perpetually present to him. The mystic John of Ruysboek wrote, 'God contemplates himself and all things in an Eternal Now.' We are held and treasured in God's memory.
*Methodist Recorder*


## Held in God's memory

• There are theologians such as Paul Tillich who hold that immortality means the continuing presence of our earthly life within the divine memory, and that is enough. With due respect to the great theologian, I doubt it, quite simply because the God in whose memory·we are held is a God of love, and love is a dynamic process; it has to engage with the other. It is of the nature of love to give and to receive, and in the act of loving, both the one who loves and the beloved are changed. If we are capable of being changed, then we can hardly be called a memory.
*'Neglected Themes in Modern Preaching'*

## Love without end

- Love is the drive to unite all that is separate in time and space and condition, and we humans meet our deaths as unfinished creatures. Our lives have been touched and changed by the love of God, so the work of making us whole will continue. Whom God loves, he loves to the end, not our end but his, and since he has no end, he must love us eternally.
*Methodist Recorder*


## New heaven and new earth

- The question of personal survival cannot be explored in isolation from the biblical claims about a new heaven and a new earth to be inaugurated by the glorious return of Christ. The whole thrust of the Gospel is that individual salvation like personal continuance is not enough. As John Baillie put it, 'There can be no complete consummation for the individual until there is consummation also for society.' It is not just the generation that happens to be on the stage of history when it reaches its goal which will be changed 'in a moment, in the twinkling of an eye'. Every generation that has ever lived must be given the opportunity to sit down at the feast of the Kingdom of Heaven. This surely is the significance of the literal meaning of 'eternal' life – the kind of life characteristic of the Age to Come.
*'Neglected Themes in Modern Preaching'*


## Disentangling eternity

- Perhaps it is those unfashionable Christian doctrines, the Last Things – death, judgement, hell and heaven – which may prove to be most immediately relevant to popular culture. C. S. Lewis was criticised for being too preoccupied with the supernatural, in the sense that the next

world loomed so large in his theology. He replied, 'How can it loom less large if it is believed in at all? If that other world is once admitted, how can it be kept in the background of our mind? How can the rest of Christianity be disentangled from it?' Christianity can only be disentangled from the dimension of the supernatural at the price of offering our society little more than a code of ethics shot through with piety.
*'Neglected Themes in Modern Preaching'*


## EVIL

### 'For Believers Fighting . . .'

• This is the title of one section of the first Methodist hymn book. And the New Testament confirms that the Christian life is warfare, grim and unrelenting. Warfare against whom? Our fathers were in no doubt – against the Devil, they would declare robustly. And there was wisdom in their giving Evil a personal name to show that there is about it the subtlety of a malevolent personality rather than the crudity of a blind irrational force.
*The Hammer of the Lord*


### The Devil's greatest achievement

• As has often been said, the Devil's greatest achievement is to convince believers that he doesn't exist. The official position of most churches on the existence of the Devil seems to be a sort of respectful agnosticism. Though references to 'sin' and 'evil' are to be found in doctrinal statements, there is no mention of the Devil, with the honourable exception of the Roman Catholic Church which refers to the Devil in one of its catechisms. One could conclude from the doctrinal statements of most

Churches that there is no Devil, yet he pops up all over the place in their hymns, sermons and prayers, and since Jesus obviously thought there was an Evil One nobody wants to take responsibility for reducing the New Testament to tatters.
*Methodist Recorder*

## Design fault

- Christians find it hard to come to terms with the Devil and recognise his true menace because they suffer from a design fault implanted in them by their Creator. God having originally made them good, they are incapable of imagining what is wholly evil, rotten through and through. They want to believe that however depraved any personality may become, some deep core of original goodness always remains intact, the mark of an original creation. So we find it hard to get our minds around unalloyed evil. Thus, the Christian poet John Milton made Satan one of the great hero figures of all literature. He is described in *Paradise Lost* as a valiant warrior, 'of mighty stature', who courageously went to war against the Almighty and remained brave and unbowed in defeat.
*'The Omega Course', Methodist Recorder*

## Pandering to our pride

- Hardly anyone believes in the Devil any more, yet everybody serves him at some point or another. No, that's wrong; we don't serve him, he serves us – pandering to our pride, convincing us that in our special case, wrong is right and lie is truth. It is this totality of distortions escalating beyond human control which constitutes what the Christian means by evil.
*Get Through Till Nightfall*

## Just the absence of good?

- Christian theologians are hopelessly at odds about the existence of evil. Some say it only has a kind of negative existence, the absence of the good, in the same way that the absence of beauty might be called ugliness. It would be convenient to hold to such an idea were it not for one stubborn fact – Jesus believed in the existence and power of Satan. We might argue that he was a man of his time in terms of earthly knowledge, but no one could claim that he lacked spiritual perception. He didn't think he was engaged in a deadly conflict against a delusion.
  *Methodist Recorder*

## The anatomy of evil

- The subtlety of evil consists in the fact it has no indè-pendent existence to forfeit. It is as insubstantial as a forbidden thought that steals into the human mind or a picture the imagination dallies with. When such thoughts and images vanish and are replaced by others, where do they go? They simply become absorbed in that darker, unacknowledged self every human possesses but tries to keep locked away. There they lie inert until human vanity, stupidity, malice, aggression and greed bring them to birth again.
  *Methodist Recorder*

## Insincere imitation

- In medieval times the Devil was known as the Ape of God. He lavished upon Christians the flattery of insincere imitation, offering them a distorting mirror in which they saw themselves as a near approximation to the character God intended them to be, but at a price which was cheaper, demanded less sacrifice and allowed more self-indulgence. If Christians took up the offer, they began to

diverge ever so slightly from the path God had chosen for them, a change of course imperceptible at first, but the angle of deflection gradually widened until they strayed into a universe whose centre was their own ego.
*Methodist Recorder*

## From the decent to the demonic

- Plain human wickedness is not hard to explain. Any old lag will tell you how he got started on what the tabloids call his 'Life of Crime'. It is the devilish twisting of our best motives that is baffling. And it is not just individuals who are capable of awful deeds, there is that collective madness which can take possession of a crowd or even a nation and drive them on to mass brutality and genocide. A whole library of books has been written since the end of the Second World War trying to explain how Germany, one of the most cultured nations on earth, became complicit in the worst excesses of Nazism. But when the psychologists, sociologists and historians have all had their say, one has an uneasy sense that a Factor X still remains unaccounted for. And evil is as accurate a word for X as any other.
*The Hammer of the Lord*

## Incomprehensible

- It is sound economics and not crude exploitation that keeps the majority of humanity below the poverty line; it is devout men, men of holy book and prayer, who roam parts of the world seeking to destroy their fellow children of God. And during the Cold War era there were generals in the Kremlin and the Pentagon, chess champions, devotees of Beethoven who doted on their children and would unhesitatingly wipe out half the population of the earth on the order of their political overlords.
*The Hammer of the Lord*

### The tendrils of evil

- The simple truth of the Second World War was that evil did not win. This is not to say that it was a morally transparent clash between our side, the Goodies, and their side, the Baddies. When the historians draw up the final balance sheet, though the preponderance of righteousness will be located on the side of the Allies, it will be seen that the tendrils of evil entwined the feet of both victors and vanquished alike. Evil did not win, but it was a close-run thing. In the end, the human spirit triumphed against all that tried to batter it into submission.
  *Starting from Scratch*

## FEAR

### Consciousness of peril

- Fear is an important element in the human psyche. Our lives are bracketed between two oblivions and haunted by fear – of enemies, of nature, of sickness, of loneliness, and supremely of death, for of all the creatures on earth, we alone know that we must die. Indeed, our experience teaches us to divide the world into safe and dangerous zones, and out of this consciousness of peril, much religion evolves.
  *Start Your Own Religion*

### Fighting against life

- There are two forces at work which can radically shape our lives: love, the Yea-sayer, and fear, the Nay-sayer. Love is the principle of life within us; fear the death bringer. To be fear-determined is to fight against life. It creates the sort of personality D. H. Lawrence described

86

as sunless, without radiance in itself and bidding to put the sun out in others.
*Get Through Till Nightfall*


## Fear not, only believe

- There is a form of fear which is biologically necessary for our survival. It is our most dramatic teacher – we touch the naked flame once and we have learned a vital lesson about fire for ever. It is our spur, we climb the near-vertical cliff because we fear the incoming tide; we risk losing our life in order to save it. But once fear ceases to be biologically essential it becomes an inhibitor, spiritually demoralising, which is why much religion is concerned with its conquest. 'Fear not, only believe,' Jesus urged his followers.
*Start Your Own Religion*


## FORGIVENESS

## Doing things together

- One of the most important things Christians do together as the Church is to demonstrate what it means to be forgiven. In believing themselves to be forgiven, Christians make the discovery that the only way they can narrow the gap between themselves and God is to move closer to their neighbour.
*Start Your Own Religion*


## Forgiveness as fact

- Jesus told his disciples, 'If you forgive the sins of any, they are forgiven; if you retain the sins of any, they are

retained.' This is not an endorsement of ecclesiastical power, giving the Church the right to exclude sinners from the benefits of salvation; it is a statement of fact. If I have done something wrong which cuts me off from the community of faith and I can find no one within it who will offer me pardon and reconciliation, then my sense of alienation deepens and I lose my belief in God's forgiveness. I do not receive because I do not ask and I do not ask because I have been treated as beyond forgiveness by those from whom almost all my knowledge of God comes.
*Let God be God*

## Christianity in a nutshell

- So central is forgiveness to Christian strategy that one could summarise Christianity as belief in a God who forgives sins through Jesus Christ our Lord.
  *Let God be God*

## God's highest power

- There is no aspect of God's being which can be dissociated from the thought of pardon. Even in the Old Testament, Jeremiah insists that the essence of God's covenant relationship with his people is 'I will forgive their iniquity and remember their sins no more.' When the prophets wished to find some way of expressing God's highest and most wonderful attributes they declared, 'Who is a God like unto thee *that pardons sins?*'
  *Let God be God*

## At peace

- To be at peace with God and to have faith that God is at peace with us is the very heart of the Christian message.
  *'Thought for the Day' – BBC Radio 4*

### Rejoining the human race

- To remain unforgiven is to be living out a sentence of death which operates by cutting us off from those who are our link with ultimate reality. This sense of alienation is deepened by fear and produces despair, 'sickness unto death' as the philosopher Kierkegaard called it. When the community accepts us and treats us forgivingly they are offering us back our humanity. It is an invitation to rejoin the human race.
  *Start Your Own Religion*

## GOD

### This remarkable idea

- We use the word 'God' so often and in so many ways without realising what a remarkable idea it stands for. There is no other construct the human mind has achieved which can account for so much: in a word, everything; life, the world, human origins and destiny. All our knowledge, hopes and fear can be organised by reference to this idea of God as a self-existent being who holds everything in existence and finally disposes of it according to his will and pleasure.
  *Start Your Own Religion*

### Shrinking God

- The biggest challenge to faith in our day doesn't come from atheists denying God but from believers diminishing him – treating him with cosy familiarity, praying to him as though he were our Old Pal upstairs or singing choruses that portray him as a benevolent simpleton.
  *Let God be God*

## Playful God

- God's glory belongs to his inner essence. We can discern useful purposes for many of God's qualities, such as his fatherhood or power or providence, but not for his glory. His glory has only one purpose, to show the playful side of his nature.
*What the Papers Didn't Say*


## Spiritual multiplication

- God is not a projection to infinity of the nicest person we've ever met. We cannot envisage him by a process of spiritual multiplication – take the sacrificial love of Mother Teresa, the eloquence of Billy Graham, the charisma of Pope John Paul II, the brain power of the cleverest professor of theology, the patience of your sainted mother, multiply by a million and you'll get some idea what God is like. He comes to meet us from the Beyond as the Wholly Other, out of dazzling darkness, as the saints put it. Therefore there is a forbidding strangeness about him which renders our cocky god-talk embarrassingly inapt.
*Let God be God*


## The godness of God

- It is conceivable that there could be a God who is not love or who is not just, but it is inconceivable there could be a God who is not holy. For in what else could his 'godness' consist?
*'The Holiness of God' – televised sermon from 'Let God be God'*

## From 'and yet' to 'therefore'

- The Bible shows the progression in the human understanding of God – God is holy said the ancients; God is
  holy *and yet* a saviour said the prophets; God is holy *and
  therefore* a saviour said Jesus.
  *'The Holiness of God' – televised sermon from 'Let God
  be God'*


## God defined

- Coventry Patmore, the Victorian poet, once defined God
  as a Synthesis of Infinity and Boundary. I suppose the
  ocean is an everyday example. The ocean is to the ordinary eye an almost limitless expanse of water, but it has a
  nearer shore, and the water line shares the same nature as
  the sea's furthermost deeps, but we can reach it. If God is
  a synthesis of infinity and boundary, who or what occupies the boundary? Who or what shares the mysterious
  nature of God and yet is within reach? Jesus, said the
  early Church.
  *Mankind My Church*


## Common journey

- When Christians claim people are converted to Jesus,
  what Jesus is converting them to is God. One practical
  result of this ought to be that we recognise as honest
  believers those whose path to God has cut through different cultural, geographical or historical terrain. The
  key question is not: do they share our faith in Jesus? but:
  do they share Jesus' faith in God?
  *Start Your Own Religion*

## Continuous creation

- God's providence is surely the conviction that the world in its tragedy and grandeur is unfolding as one great Divine creative act. It is the confidence that all will be well in the end, not that his purpose is transparent in his willingness to do this individual act rather than another one at our earnest urging. Only in view of its final purpose does the world make sense.

  *'Neglected Themes in Modern Preaching'*

## Narrow tolerances

- Natural theology is concerned with the evidences for God's existence in the created order, but it could equally be argued that the purpose of creation is to protect us from the impact of a reality so intense we would be destroyed by it. Demosthenes wrote, 'If you cannot bear the candle, how will you face the sun?' Our lives are lived within the narrowest of tolerances – if our temperatures rise or fall by a few degrees we die. Too much sound or too much silence and we go mad. How could we withstand the unmistakable presence of God? A West African creation story makes the point perfectly. In the beginning God was pure naked God and human beings were afraid to go near him. So God covered himself with the mantle of Creation, rivers in which they could fish, soil they could cultivate. Forests in which they could hunt. So human beings lost their fear of approaching God – and God, so the story ends, was as happy as a dog with fleas.

  *Mankind My Church*

## Naming God

- Again and again, Jesus said, 'Father'. It is the last and final word in the naming of God. You can't get beyond it or behind it, transform it into a more accessible metaphor

or popularise it. That's it; the terminus in the human understanding of God.
*Bible Reflections Round the Christian Year*

## Absence as a form of presence

- The psychologist William James was once asked whether he believed in God and he answered that he wasn't sure, but the issue seemed to him like a ticking clock in the room in which he worked. He was quite unaware of it until it stopped, and then he heard a strange silence. So he thought there was something at the back of his life of which he was outwardly heedless but inwardly aware. At the deepest levels of our being there is something in us which resonates to the voice of God as a flower turns its face to the sun or a divining rod quivers in the presence of water in the desert.
*Bible Reflections Round the Christian Year*

## By divine permission

- This biblical theme of God's absence ('Truly, you are a God that hides yourself!' protests Job) means many things; one is to give a cutting edge to our social action. The fact that God, as it were, steps out of the picture, enables us to invest our fellow human beings with ultimate significance. I can *see* God in the outcast, the prisoner and the afflicted because I can see him nowhere else. I am a humanist by divine permission.
*Mankind My Church*

## Half-remembered words

- Christians nourish their spiritual life by those disciplines of religion they go through almost as a matter of routine; the half-remembered phrases of a thousand prayers; the

rich imagery of many hymns; sermons galore that seem to have passed in through one ear and out at the other with the odd illustration sticking in their memories; snatches of familiar Bible passages. They sink deep into the psyche but are capable of being triggered in moments of crisis.
*Bible Reflections Round the Christian Year*

## Holy love

- 'God is love' is a sublime truth, but it is not the whole Gospel. If you want the Gospel in a sound-bite, try this – God is holy love. That's it. As P. T. Forsyth pointed out, God is not just our loving Father, he is our Holy Father, and the distinction in action between the two dramatises the difference between forgiveness and redemption.
*'Neglected Themes in Modern Preaching'*

## From specific to general

- In their thinking about God, the Jews moved from the specific to the general – from *their* God backwards to the notion of God as creator and outwards to God as sovereign; much as Paul in the Letter to the Colossians moved backwards from redemption to creation and outwards from personal saviour to cosmic Christ.
*Let God be God*

## Would the God of Jesus do that?

- The Bible is the record of the long search to discover the rules by which God uses his power. And it was Jesus who brought those rules into the full light of day in a number of acted parables. And he did so with such authority that afterwards, when his followers were uncertain whether God was responsible for some world-shaking event, they

found themselves asking, 'Would the God of Jesus do that?'
*Bible Reflections Round the Christian Year*


## Jesusolatry

- Without in any way diminishing the centrality of Jesus, we must beware of a certain Jesusolatry which insists that what we *do* know about Jesus is all we *can* know about God. We have the authority of Jesus himself that this will not do. 'Don't look at me,' he declared. 'Look at him.' He would not allow himself to stand in God's light. We Christians need from time to time a dose of thorough-going monotheism to clean out our clogged theological systems. And who better to provide it than Jews and Muslims whose fierce protection of God's holiness and unknowability is one of the religious glories of a secular age? The Jews, of course, have the additional qualification that they taught the young Jesus about God, and certainly made a good job of it.
*A Week in the Life of God*


## Held by God

- We profess to worship a God who holds the whole universe neatly in the palm of His hand, yet in our moods of black despair we imagine that He has lost control of the speck on which we are standing. Happily, we are always wrong.
*Doris Laird, 'Colin Morris, Modern Missionary'*

## Silent appeal

- God's patience is just another word for his grace, which batters down no doors, doesn't take the biggest hall in town or announce its presence with heavenly fireworks. What did Isaiah predict about the way the Messiah would behave? 'He will not strive nor cry aloud, nor make his voice heard in the streets.' Grace operates only by the power of silent appeal. A seed is not driven upwards through the ground by the violence of natural forces, it is coaxed out by the warmth of the sun. The delicacy with which the sun's rays encourage the plant to blossom is a model of God's grace.
  *Let God be God*

## The unexpected

- Grace is that unexpected element we can neither command nor deserve which enters a situation from outside and seeks saving possibilities within it.
  *Start Your Own Religion*

## Gift or demand?

- The Victorian preacher C. H. Spurgeon describes how he went with money from his church collection to help pay the rent of a poor woman of the parish. He knocked again and again but failed to get any response. The woman was inside, all right, but she didn't open the door because she thought it was the rent man. The knock signalled a gift; she thought it was a demand.
  *Starting from Scratch*

## Unsnarl the log-jams

- You can't write off the most intractable political conflict as insoluble. There is a creative factor at work in human affairs, call it what you will, I call it the grace of God, which when the time is right, can help to unsnarl log-jams and span unbridgeable gulfs, causing the bitterest of opponents to have changes of heart.
  *'Thought for the Day'* – BBC Radio 4

## HOLINESS

### Unapproachable mystery

- The word holiness means to separate sharply, to cut. And at first hearing, 'holy' seems a cold word; there attaches to it the frigidity of starlight, the remoteness of endless space; infinite distance, unapproachable mystery. Jesus warmed it, revolutionised our understanding of it. He was, said the Gospels, the holy one of God. In him, holiness confronts us as grace.
  *Starting from Scratch*

### Exuberance

- The later Biblical images of the way of holiness are not frosty and remote but boisterous and joyous and noisy – pictures of the lame leaping like deer, the tongue of the dumb shouting, of happy clamour, of feasting in the kingdom of heaven. Holiness is the happiness of those who are at peace with God.
  *Starting from Scratch*

## Holiness as moral energy

- In the old religion, the believer confronted by the ineffable holiness of the deity was seized by terror and sought to placate it by non-rational responses – human sacrifice, magic, taboo. But the genius of the prophets was to shift the centre of gravity of religion from the magical to the moral. 'Rend your hearts and not your garments,' says Joel. 'He leads me,' says the Psalmist, 'into the paths of righteousness' – not into esoteric rites. Isaiah's reaction on coming face to face with the Holy God in the temple was to cry, 'I am a man of unclean lips and dwell amongst a people of unclean lips!' God's holiness inspires ethical renewal and moral regeneration.
  *Starting from Scratch*

## From holiness to action

- The shocking particularity of God's love reaches its climax when the Holy One who is in all, through all and over all, becomes incarnate in a tiny backwater of the Roman Empire, leaves footprints in the sand and discarded bandages in an empty tomb. And the practicality of the service he demands is illustrated in those anecdotes about everyday life we call the parables of the Kingdom, thus proving that Christianity isn't theory but the art of life seeking an ever higher and better technique.
  *Out of Africa's Crucible*

## HOLY SPIRIT

### Festival in the Fog

- Pentecost can easily become the Festival in the Fog; it lends itself to vagueness. The problem is that of the three persons of the Trinity, the Holy Spirit is the most difficult to visualise. 'God the Father', that's a strong image; God the Son? Well, we have Jesus to feed our imaginations on; but the Holy Spirit? What's there? The very word Spirit suggests formlessness, swirling mist. And the old traditional term, Holy Ghost, is even vaguer; you can't strike up much of a relationship with a ghost. But there is another traditional image of the Holy Spirit: Fire. There's nothing vague about that.

*Start Your Own Religion*

## Casting fire on the earth

• Lorenzo de' Medici was a great showman and impresario in the sixteenth century who laid on great displays and spectacles at religious festivals. One Whitsun he surpassed himself when he re-enacted the first Pentecost in one of Florence's historic churches. Apparently with a great roar, tongues of real flame descended on the heads of the Apostles, but then got out of control. It burned the clothes off the actors, set ablaze the scenery, and then the heat cracked the walls of the church, and a howling gale fanned the flames, destroying several nearby buildings. Lorenzo's Pentecostal flames consumed the church. There's a moral there.

*Sermon – Wesley's Chapel*

## The Spirit's scope

• We talk about the Church possessing the Spirit; it is the precise reverse, the Spirit possesses the Church. The Church does not contain the Spirit as a vessel contains fuel; the Spirit contains the Church as an ocean contains fish. The Spirit's scope is more majestic than that of the Church. It is the Spirit in the beginning which broods upon primeval chaos and brings the world into being; it

is the Spirit which at the end shows us the Holy City
Jerusalem coming down out of heaven from God.
*Sermon – Wesley's Chapel*


## World changing and life transforming

• Those who expect the presence of the Spirit to increase
and deepen personal religion are right. That's what
happened at Pentecost. But something else happened too.
This collection of individuals who spoke many languages
and came from different places were moulded together,
welded by the fire of the Spirit into a new community
with one heart and one soul, not just for pious purposes
but to create the microcosm of a new social order – they
abandoned private property, showed fresh care for the
poor and a new respect for slaves. Pentecostal fire fused
together the personal and social dimensions of religion
to turn the faith into a world-changing as well as life-
transforming force.
*The Hammer of the Lord*


## God's perfect taste

• The biblical epic of creation depicts a scene of primeval
chaos – darkness, formlessness and mystery. But above
the ceaseless roar of clashing systems, the brooding Spirit
pauses, pondering how he will apply the supreme
creative energy of his love. God's perfect taste is brought
to bear on the imperfect material of the universe; the
Spirit draws out its latent possibilities, the beauty,
wonder and variety of life.
*Bible Reflections Round the Christian Year*

## From Babel to Pentecost

- The story of the fall of the Tower of Babel describes a human condition totally without hope, our spiritual language reduced to a cacophony of meaningless sounds. If it stood alone in the Bible without a sequel, humanity could only be resigned to its fate. But it was at Pentecost that the curse of Babel was cancelled as 'all present began to speak' in a new language, the language of doxology – causing the Lord's name to be praised. The infinite distance between God and humankind which the Tower of Babel failed to bridge was spanned in and through the Spirit of Jesus.
  *Things Shaken, Things Unshaken*

## The New Israel

- Out of Pentecost emerges not just a common language but a society without frontiers, the New Israel, whose citizens are drawn from every corner of the earth. Unlike other nations, its citizens are called and chosen rather than thrown together by biological accident. Whereas the other nations are agglomerations of great power, the New Israel glories in its powerlessness, choosing suffering rather than self-interest as its key signature.
  *Church and Challenge in a New Africa*

## Christlikeness

- God as Spirit spoke through the prophets, and possessed Jesus so completely that it didn't seem too fulsome to speak of the self-revelation of God; it was this same Spirit which at Pentecost imbued the apostles with Christlikeness, and this same Spirit which is firing our imagination to this very moment.
  *Lecture, 'The Unfinished Revolution' – Swanwick*

## What remains

- Paul assures the Christians at Corinth that when all else passes, faith, hope and love abide. These are the essential dimensions of the Christian life. Hope is possible because the one who follows the way of Christ has faith that there is no situation, however unpromising, which is impervious to love. Faith defines the Church, love holds it together; hope keeps it in existence.
*Bugles in the Afternoon*

## Adding zest to faith

- Love and faith have greater importance than hope. God's love is given to us in Jesus Christ; that is a dead certainty. Faith is our recognition and acceptance of that love, and is obviously next in importance. But hope is still essential even though it cannot have the same degree of certainty as the other two, otherwise the word would lose its meaning. Without hope, faith would harden into a certainty that renders unbelief impossible or insane, for who needs faith in what has been proved beyond a shadow of a doubt? Yet though hope is the lowest in the hierarchy of Christian virtues, it adds tang to the rest, making the Christian life an adventure.
*Mankind My Church*

## The command to hope

- The Talmud tells of a rabbi who wondered what sort of questions he might be asked at the Last Judgement. Some of the commandments were obvious and concerned honesty in business, strict observance of the Torah and the search for wisdom. One question was startling

because it seemed to embody a contradiction – 'Have you hoped for the Messiah?' How can one be *commanded* to hope, any more than they can be told to love or ordered to have faith? Yet this paradox has haunted Jewish history and is as near to an explanation as one is likely to get for the extraordinary fact that the Jewish people have survived at all, bound together by nothing more substantial than a dream turned into a commandment.
*Unyoung, Uncoloured, Unpoor*

## A saving possibility

- The saving possibility in desperate times is the presence of agents of hope who for much of the time bash away with the proverbial feather-duster at all too solid rocks. But when the moment of crisis comes, they constitute themselves into a body of people prepared to risk all and give all in order to transform a hopeless situation by providing a hospitable environment for some new initiative.
*The Hammer of the Lord*

## The ethics of hope

- We can respond to our fellow human beings in any one of three ways. We can obey the law: do unto others as they have done to you. These are the ethics of retribution, calculated to ensure that nothing changes. There is a higher law that runs: do unto others as you would like them to do to you. These are the ethics of optimism, a great step forward but demanding more of unregenerate human nature than can be realistically expected. The third law embodies the essence of the Gospel: do unto others as Christ has done to you. These are the ethics of hope. They demand that we offer others what Christ has offered us: sacrifice, acceptance and renewal through suffering. They derive their power from a transaction in

which we can expect everything from Christ but need nothing from others.
*The Hammer of the Lord*


## Faith, love and hope

• Hope is possible because the one who follows the way of Christ has faith that there is no human situation, however unpromising, which is impervious to love. Here are the three pillars on which the Kingdom of God is raised in the life of the individual believer: faith venturing beyond the unprovable, love forgiving the unpardonable, and hope remaining undimmed against all odds.
*Bugles in the Afternoon*


## HUMOUR

### Biblical wit

• In the Old Testament there is a rich vein of mocking humour attributed to God. In one of the greatest of all religious poems, the Book of Job, God bombards Job with a torrent of barbed witticisms. Then there is the discussion between God and Abraham about the birth of Isaac, whose very name means 'laughter' – the point being that God has played a joke on Sarah who to her astonishment has become pregnant at an advanced age. There are Elijah's knockabout tirades against the priests of Baal on Carmel, and in Deuteronomy, the very book of the Bible which warns us against taking God's name in vain, he is described as winking and giggling. In one of the most surprising images of the Bible, the Book of Psalms describes God sitting in heaven roaring with laughter. There is much biblical evidence of a laughing God.
*God in the Shower*

## Misuse of words

- Life has both serious and funny aspects and we tend to pigeonhole religion in the category of the solemn. But the terms 'funny' and 'serious' are not opposites. The opposite of 'funny' is 'unfunny'; the opposite of 'serious' is 'trivial'. So a subject can be both 'serious' and 'funny' at the same time. It was G. K. Chesterton who said that the acid test of a good religion was whether we could laugh about it.
  *God in the Shower*

## Divine jocularity

- If the grand rule of theology is that we must not deny to God any qualities we human beings demonstrate at our highest and best, then we must assume that God has a sense of humour. He needs one. To be impermissibly anthropomorphic about him, there must be occasions when he doesn't know whether to laugh or cry at the antics we humans get up to.
  *A Week in the Life of God*

## The vulgarity of Jesus

- Jesus was a countryman with a rough tongue and a distinctive brogue. The earthiness of rustic wit runs through many of his sayings. He described rotting corpses burying one another, pearls flung before ritually unclean animals, dirty cups being washed on the outside leaving the inside greasy, open-flame lamps being hidden under inflammable straw mattresses – images that originated from a richly comic and vulgar imagination – 'vulgar' in its literal sense, 'of the people'.
  *A Week in the Life of God*

## A rich vein of humour

- A bishop has condemned the Monty Python film, *The Life of Brian*. 'The story of our redemption is too serious a matter for ribald comedy,' he said. Leaving aside the fact that the film is not about Jesus of Nazareth but about a fictional character called Brian, my contention is that no subject is too serious for comedy, though there are occasions when comedy would be an insensitive or inappropriate way of dealing with it. Surely the Holocaust is the limiting case, and yet a rich vein of humour came out of the death camps, and the survivors have recorded the funny stories inmates told one another. Mind you, they have the exclusive right to such humour. Thus Rabbi Lionel Gryn who had first-hand experience of the death camps told the story of one Jewish inmate of Belsen saying to another, 'Given a life like this, it would be better for a Jew not to have been born at all.' 'True,' the other replied, 'but how many Jews get to be that lucky? Maybe, one in ten thousand!'
*Debate about 'The Life of Brian' – Oxford Union*


## The last line of defence

- Victor Frankel, an Austrian Jewish psychiatrist, wrote of his experiences in a Nazi extermination camp. He describes how the inmates passed beyond terror to the point where every morning when the commandant appeared with the dreaded list in his hand of those chosen for the death chambers, the victims found themselves laughing out loud at the portentousness of this daily ritual and the officer's ludicrous mispronunciation of their names. Frankel insisted it wasn't hysteria, but a strategy; the only way the children of God, brutalised like animals, could assert their humanity. For who has the last word, the one who has life or death control over others or those who can laugh at him?
*A Week in the Life of God*

## Serious comedy

- Comedy itself is a serious subject. This is because it offers a perspective on life, if somewhat distorted; a way of looking at reality, however squint-eyed; a weighing of moral and social values in the balance, even though the scales are wonky. We can only make a joke about serious things, for frivolous things are already a joke. There can be no humour where everything is serious or everything is funny.
  *Debate about 'The Life of Brian' – Oxford Union*

## Divine comedy

- When Dante finally arrives in Paradise after his arduous climb out of the Inferno, he hears choirs of angels singing praises to the Trinity and says, 'It seemed like the laughter of the universe.' It is significant that he called his epic work which embraces the universal condition of the human soul, *The Divine Comedy*.
  *Starting from Scratch*

## Pancake Day

- Shrove Tuesday is an important day in the Church's calendar because it serves to remind us that religion is meant to be enjoyed rather than endured.
  *God in the Shower*

- We need a comic perspective on religion to preserve us from making idiots of ourselves by according our self-made idols undue respect.
  *Start Your Own Religion*

# IDOLATRY

## Object of terror

- The Hebrew words translated as 'idol' in the King James Bible mean 'object of terror', 'thing of nought', 'abominable', and 'cause of grief'. And in the New Testament, idolaters are consigned to the less than admirable company of liars, dogs, extortioners and adulterers. And yet . . . as soon as we try to grasp through our senses the nature of reality, we have created an idol, even if it is only a theological idea. Without it we would be adrift with no compass in an endless ocean. Though the Jews proclaimed their loathing of any pictorial representations of God, human nature and the character of human language defeated them. Hence, in the same scriptures which ban the making of graven images, God is described as walking in the Garden of Eden. He stretches his arm, his voice shakes the cedars, and according to the psalmist, he can be tasted and found good. To forbid the making of pictures about God would be to rule out any thoughts of him at all, because we think in pictures.
*Starting from Scratch*

## Human images are best

- Idolotory inevitably results from thinking in pictures rather than abstract principles. Take one of the gods of the philosophers, say, Cosmic Essence. Close your eyes and try to imagine a cosmic essence; or there is the God of the Platonists, the Absolute Unknown. What can come into your mind other than a total blank? So if mental pictures of God are inevitable, then by far the best and safest are those which are cast in the form of human personality and qualities. Hence, God as king, father, mother, lover, friend. These will inevitably be the main sources of our pictures of God.
*Start Your Own Religion*

## Manufactured gods

- The prophet Micah warns, 'Do not worship gods you have made yourself' (5.13). Some of the most potent gods of modern times are the products of human ingenuity – political gods such as nationalism, fascism, or even democracy; intellectual gods such as scientism, hedonism or even consumerism. The Bible warns that we tend to grow like the gods we have manufactured. Wrote the psalmist, 'Their idols are silver and gold, the work of men's hands. They have mouths but they speak not; eyes they have, but see not, and they that make them become like them.'
*Bible Reflections Round the Christian Year*

- Jesus was always conscious of the danger of his followers turning him into an idol, which is why he commanded them to look beyond himself to his Father. According to the fourth Gospel, he warned his disciples, 'He who believes in me does not believe in me but in him who sent me.' And Paul looked to the time when God would be all in all, with even the Son in subjection to him.
*Start Your Own Religion*

## IMAGINATION

## Walking his way

- The imagination is the seat of personal faith. Evangelicals sing choruses about Jesus coming into their heart, but that's just a figure of speech; it is their imagination he takes over. From there, he can possess their wills so that they start to walk his way.
*Methodist Recorder*

## All possibilities

- We talk about figments of the imagination, as though they are fantasy; this is because in ordinary speech we assume that 'imagined' means the same thing as 'unreal'. In fact, the world of the imagination is real alright, and humans spend much of their time there. In fact, it rules their lives. By the power of the imagination, humans have created whole civilisations. All the wonders of art, literature, music and science come into being because they can imagine what was not already there. We can imagine things being different from what they are now, better or worse, brighter or grimmer, lovelier or uglier, nobler or more depraved. All the possibilities of life are contained in the imagination, God and the Devil, Heaven and Hell. Jesus and other religious prophets offered their followers visions of a future different from all that had gone before, a new, perfect creation.
*Methodist Recorder*

## Vivid imagery

- Though Christians have traditionally distrusted the imagination, without it, their sacred books would be just dead words from a lost era. The New Testament writers were highly imaginative. They took a Galilean peasant about whom almost nothing was known – even his physical appearance was a mystery – and they presented him to their contemporaries in a series of vivid images – The Light of the World, The Lamb of God, The Door, The Bread of Life, the True Vine, The Good Shepherd, The Alpha and Omega, the Resurrection and the Life, King of Kings and Lord of Lords. These metaphors are not just verbal pictures; they mediate power as well as description. Here was rich material for the imagination of Christians to work on so that they could make connections between Jesus' world and their own.
*God-in-a-Box*

## Visualisation

- The unremarked factor in the decline of organised religion has been the withering of the human imagination. One obvious reason is the spread of television which short-circuits the imagination by presenting us with explicit experiences and ideas we would otherwise have to visualise for ourselves. This is why many BBC radio fans insist they prefer radio because the pictures are better.
  *The Christian Conundrum – BBC Radio 2*

## JESUS CHRIST

### A God named Jack

- It is much easier to believe in a God-like being called Christ imprisoned in a stained glass window above the altar than in a Messiah called Jack or its first century equivalent, Joshua, who lived in the next hovel, drank at the same well and used the same outside privy.
  *Bible Reflections Round the Christian Year*

### The Big Idea

- Christmas is about the arrival of the Messiah, and there's an incident in Matthew's Gospel where the disciples of John the Baptist enquire of Jesus whether or not he is the Messiah – 'Are you the one we are expecting or should we look for another?' In his reply, Jesus doesn't mention star, stable or wise men. He says, 'Tell John that the blind see, the lame walk, the deaf hear and the poor have some good news.' That's the true message, the Big Idea of Christmas.
  *Bible Reflections Round the Christian Year*

## Celluloid Saviour

- If the theologians have had great difficulty in finding some way of describing Jesus that took full account of both his divinity and his humanity, it is understandable that when the first films were made of Christ's life, Hollywood did not know what to make of him, so it approached the task with excessive reverence. The actor who played Jesus was not named, nor was his face ever fully seen. He had to be of blameless moral reputation. Totally immune from any of the usual Hollywood scandals, he was commanded to give no press interviews. He must not be seen in real life as an ordinary human being with tastes and opinions, who might sweat in front of reporters or make grammatical mistakes. For as Cecil B. de Mille said, it was unthinkable that the Son of God should split an infinitive.
*Wrestling with an Angel*

## Love and the lover

- There is one great difference between the forms of knowledge such as science and philosophy offer and those revealed by Jesus. Take Descartes or Freud or Einstein out of the picture and we might still have their ideas; their discoveries stand in their own light; someone sometime would have come up with them. But you cannot have the gospel without Jesus, for the simple reason that love has no meaning in isolation from the lover; it doesn't linger on as an abstract quality, however noble. Einstein could not be the Special Theory of Relativity in the way that Christ himself is Christianity. A personality came into the world who did not merely point towards but embodied God's new creation.
*Bible Reflections Round the Christian Year*

## His fate in our hands

- The word become flesh is a tremendous demonstration of
  faith: not our faith in God, that waxes and wanes, but
  God's faith in us, entrusting his fate and his kingdom into
  our shaky hands. It is the ultimate cosmic wager; God
  banking that we will not let him down.
  *Mankind My Church*

## The inner vein of truth

- The Old Testament prophets predicted the appearance of
  one who would embody God's will as fully as a human
  being could: the Messiah, in fact. God's self-disclosure
  became increasingly specific, personal, even local, until,
  so Christians claim, the inner vein of divine truth began
  to break surface, a particular human life becoming transparent to the divine will. The one for whom the Jews still
  wait, Christians insist has arrived.
  *Starting from Scratch*

## Inevitable outcome

- Jesus took God with utter seriousness, gave absolute
  form to the religion the prophets taught. Jesus' kingdom
  collided with the empire of Caesar and the priesthood of
  Caiaphas. Since God had ruled out any arbitrary imposi-
  tion of his will on humanity, the outcome was inevitable.
  *Mankind My Church*

## As good as the next man

- When I left theological college I had a landlady who like
  most Yorkshire women was very house-proud. Every
  Monday morning she hung out her washing and against
  the grey pit slag heaps her whites glowed. One night it

snowed and against the pristine whiteness of the snow her washing lost some its radiance. I'm as good as the next man unless the next man happens to be Jesus Christ.
*Bible Reflections Round the Christian Year*

## Shaking the earth

- The New Testament image of the Christ who sneaks back into history like a thief in the night well illustrates the balance that has to be struck in our thinking between the Christ who is always encountering us anonymously and the Christ who will also one day be manifest in glory; the Christ who as Spirit stirs our hearts now and the Christ who as King will shake the earth at the end.
*Mankind My Church*

## The tearing of the veil

- According to Matthew's Gospel, the veil of the great temple in Jerusalem was torn apart at the moment Jesus died. What might this mean? Surely, it symbolised the end of God's preoccupation with one people. Jesus lived a Jew but he did not die one; he died a man. And in dying as a public spectacle, he rendered obsolete all concepts of religion based on special rites or sacred elites. It is as a human being that anyone is saved where he or she stands, they do not need to fight their way to some special sanctuary. Salvation for all! – is the message of the rending of the Temple veil.
*Mankind My Church*

## Brighter than the sun

- Again, according to Matthew, another momentous happening at the time of Jesus' death was the sun veiling its face. For natural man, the sun was the ultimate power of the universe and the source of all life; but the sun veiled its face to acknowledge that an even greater power had been revealed. As Paul puts it, the first Adam was a living soul, like the rest of creation obviously dependent on the sun for his existence; but the second Adam was a *life-giving* spirit – a new form of power driving through and beyond nature.

*Mankind My Church*

## Tiptoeing through a minefield

• The Jesus of the Gospels seems to sail through the upper air, serenely isolated from the politics of his day, exchanging repartee about worship, theology and personal morality. In fact, he lived at the heart of a battlefield across which a running war was fought for much of his lifetime. Is it not odd that according to the Gospels he was asked to pronounce on such rarefied issues as the heavenly marital state of a woman with a number of earthly husbands, but no one asked him the more obvious and urgent question of whether the Zealots were justified in creating havoc by their violent attacks on the Romans? After all, the only hard fact about his life corroborated by non-Christian historians of the time is that he was a Jewish nationalist executed for stirring up rebellion against the Roman occupiers of his homeland. That may not have been true, but it defies belief that the issue never crossed his mind and that he did not discuss it with his disciples. My guess is that the early Church knew much more about Jesus than they let on in the Gospels.

*Unyoung, Uncoloured, Unpoor*

## Rendering to Caesar

• When Jesus was asked whether it was lawful to pay tribute to Caesar he is said to have taken a coin with

Caesar's inscription on it and said, 'Render to Caesar what is Caesar's and to God what is God's.' This is taken to mean that he was not guilty of sedition; the Jews could pay tribute to Rome. But one only has to ask, what in the eyes of a devout Jew belonged to Caesar in the Holy Land? The answer is – nothing. The Romans had invaded the land of a free people and ruled by force. Throughout their long history, the Jews never wavered in their belief that everything which touched their lives, their land, the people and its wealth belonged to God alone. If God had his due, Caesar would get nothing. So I read that as a subversive answer.

*Unyoung, Uncoloured, Unpoor*


## JUDGEMENT

### Love as wrath

- We misunderstand scripture when we transliterate the word 'wrath' into its human equivalent, anger, whereas when used of God, it has nothing to do with turbulent emotion. St Augustine in a lovely phrase wrote that God's wrath does not disturb the tranquillity of his mind. There is no heat, fire, or aggression in it. There is a pregnant phrase in the Gospel after Peter has betrayed Jesus. The verse runs: 'And the Lord turned and looked on Peter, and Peter knew.' No condemnation, no animus, no heated harangue, just sorrow apprehended as wrath. Because God is always and all-through Love, even his wrath is an expression of his love; its purpose is to save, not to destroy.

*Judges' service – Liverpool Cathedral*

## Merciful discrimination

- Bartimaeus receives his sight, the leper is cleansed, the epileptic boy is healed, Jairus' daughter is raised from the dead. So far as we know, Jesus made no further appeal that they should become his disciples. At other times his demand is radical – 'Leave your nets!' or 'Sell all you have and give to the poor!' Why the difference? Jesus always showed a merciful discrimination. He knew what was in human nature.
  *Let God be God*


## The final word

- A Last Judgment means that there is nothing more to be said; God has spoken his final word. In the coming of Christ the Last Judgment is on. We are up against him in a way that could not be more final. 'Now is the judgment of this world,' said Jesus on his way to Jerusalem as his passion and death began. 'Now shall the prince of this world be cast out.'
  *The Hammer of the Lord*


## Silent forces

- Imagine a man whose only desire in life is to lie on the beach all day and do nothing, even though there are many things he ought to be doing. As he lies there, no voice from heaven says, 'Come on old chap, you have a destiny, get on the move!' But all around him are silent forces in conspiracy to get him moving. They work a kind of judgment on him. Silently the sun goes down and he's got to move or freeze; silently, time rolls on and he's got to move or starve; silently, the tide creeps in, he's got to move or drown. There is also a principle of retribution in Scripture. It's not a blind, irrational force; it's the

irresistible outworking of a moral order vested in the holiness of God.
*The Hammer of the Lord*

## The voice of judgement

- The voice of almighty God in judgement is heard not booming from beyond the stars but in the cry of the hungry for bread, the downtrodden for dignity and the victim for justice. He keeps silent so that they can speak for him. That is a quite astonishing and frightening thought – the Eternal One who inhabits the Heaven of Heavens and rides upon the whirlwind, before whom all the nations are as a drop in a bucket, keeps silence so that you can hear the cry of the downtrodden. They speak for him. In their wail of anguish there is more divine judgement upon us than torrents of heavenly denunciation.
*Let God be God*

## Against the rub of the universe

- George Bernard Shaw, asked by a young man for good advice on living, said, 'Find out which way the universe is going and go with it.' 'Come, inherit the Kingdom prepared for you from the foundation of the world,' says the great King in the parable. That's the way the universe is going. We are structured for the Kingdom as the eye is for light or the heart for love. To try to live any other way is to move against the grain of the universe, and that is fighting one's way in the teeth of God's love.
*Start Your Own Religion*

## Truth as Light

- According to John's Gospel Jesus makes two affirmations that seem to be contradictory: 'I came not to judge the

world but to save the world' and 'For judgement I came into the world.' How are these two statements to be reconciled? The Gospel does it through the image of Jesus as the Light of the world – 'This is the judgement, that light is come into the world and men love the darkness rather than light.' It is the notion of judgement as an inevitable by-product of Jesus' saving presence – judgement as exposure to the truth. We can get by in the semi-gloom with our deceptions, illusions and half-lies; then light comes into the world and we are utterly unmasked.
*Bible Reflections Round the Christian Year*

## Letting things take their course

* One of the most disturbing stories in the Gospels is that of the healing of the ten lepers. Jesus heals all ten, but only one, a Samaritan, returns to thank him. Why did Jesus accept the situation without comment? Why did he not call the nine back and remonstrate with them, pointing out what a miracle had been done for them? He leaves it at that, accepting their attitude. Is not the moral of the story that if we are unmoved by God, the danger is not that in his anger he may consume us but accept his failure with us without protest? He confronts us, we make our choice, and in judging him, we are judged.
*Sermon*

## JUSTICE

* Justice is the hard skeleton which gives shape to community life, the framework within which fellowship can grow. It is about keeping my self-assertiveness in check so that it conflicts as little as possible with yours.
*Things Shaken, Things Unshaken*

## Neither angels nor devils

- The Christian faith is realistic about the average person's capacity for justice. It assumes tolerable decency as a general human characteristic. The vast majority of people are neither angels nor devils. Not being angels, they are prone to put their own interests first so power enters the equation as the measure of constraint needed to see others get their due. But they are not devils either. They have the will and desire to settle most disputes by mutual agreement, so for much of the time we can harmonise our claims on others with theirs on us.
  *Things Shaken, Things Unshaken*

## No notice

- Justice takes no notice of the power, wealth and wisdom of those who seek it, though there is one over-riding consideration. Any inequality in the distribution of social values must be exercised in favour of the less advantaged. This was the constant theme of the Old Testament prophets.
  *Church and Challenge in a New Africa*

## Bias towards the poor

- The Bible's view of justice is nothing like so simple as that of Aristotle, 'To each his due!' The snag with this definition is that I am always alert to circumstances in which I get less than my due. But I may not be equally sensitive to the fact that you are being given less than what's rightfully yours. The prophets declaimed that God was angry with princes and kings because they turned away the poor from their doors. Biblical justice always has a bias towards the poor. As Moffatt's translation puts it, 'He has torn imperial powers from their thrones, but the humble have been lifted up high.'
  *Mankind My Church*

## Transparency

- The corruptive effects of power demand that what the State does must always be under public scrutiny. The people must be able to see justice manifestly being done in order that they will reverence as well as obey the law. In a democracy, a law the people obey but do not respect will not long survive.
  *Church and Challenge in a New Africa*

- The Hebrew word for justice is *tsedeqh*, translated as 'righteousness' in older versions of the Bible. It means more than making the punishment fit the crime; it is putting right what was wrong; it is a political strategy as well as an individual virtue.
  *Sermon*

## God as Judge

- 'Shall not the Judge of all the earth do right?' This rhetorical question was directed by Abraham to God and marks a landmark in the development of the Judaeo-Christian religion. This was a time when ancient peoples were in thrall to gods noted for their capriciousness, who at whim might bless their devotees with a harvest or in a bad mood blast them with thunderbolts. And then, amongst the Jews, there dawned a different perception of God: God not as Absolute Monarch, Heavenly Tyrant or Celestial Dictator but as Judge. And that image encapsulated a revolutionary understanding of God's nature. The Jewish patriarchs refused to believe that God was totally unpredictable. He was, they came to believe, morally consistent. There was rhyme and reason for his actions. He was prepared to subject himself to the moral order he himself had ordained.
  *Judges' service – Liverpool Cathedral*

## Deterrence

- A deterrent sentence is one that sends out a signal warning those thinking of committing the same offence what they may expect from the courts. It may be an understandable reaction in a time of rising crime rates, but deterrence should be an affront to the Christian conscience because it means loading upon one offender a punishment related not solely to what he or she has actually done, but also to what others might have it in mind to do. Indeed, there is no necessary relationship between guilt and deterrence. One could boil in oil an innocent person chosen at random as a warning to villains what they can expect if caught. It might be effective, but it would not be just. I would be happier if politicians talked less about law and order and more about justice.
  *Get Through Till Nightfall*

## Just deserts

- Though the concept of giving someone their 'just deserts', neither more nor less, sounds impossibly old-fashioned, it is in fact a Christian response to an offender because it treats him or her as a human being rather than an example or a scapegoat.
  *'Thought for the Day'* – BBC Radio 4

## Persistent virtues

- Underlying the varieties of customs and law to be found in different societies and cultures, there are certain basic qualities, which, however disguised, must persist because any tolerable life is impossible without them. Justice is pre-eminent, for without it society would be in constant turmoil; but there is also courage, integrity and truthfulness. Truth keeps us in touch with reality, and it is

integrity or constancy which guarantees our identity from day to day.
*Start Your Own Religion*

## The primacy of the inferior

- For I saw that the genius of Christianity is that it exalts those who in the eyes of the world are inferior or backward or despicable. It proclaims not the equality of the inferior but his primacy.
*The Hour After Midnight*

## KINGDOM OF GOD

## Diminished vision

- Whenever the followers of Jesus have abandoned this sense of the primacy of the Kingdom they have lost vision and purpose; there has been a scaling down of their perception from Christlikeness universalised, which is what the Kingdom is, to Christlikeness particularised which is what the Church is. God's aim is not to build stronger churches but to redeem creation.
*Methodist Recorder*

## Variations on a theme

- The Gospel makes it clear that the quest for the Kingdom comes before all else. All our other loyalties, to the church, to the nation, to the family even, are secondary to that one. It was clearly Jesus' master-obsession; it dominated his thinking, his prayers and his preaching. If Wesley was a man of one book, Jesus was a man of one sermon. The Kingdom, always the Kingdom – a hundred variations on the same theme.
*Sermon – Wesley's Chapel*

## A king without a kingdom

- So closely intertwined are Jesus and the Kingdom that
  to come to terms with Jesus alone is to make a half-
  discovery; it is to acknowledge a king without a kingdom; it is reverence without responsibility. On the other
  hand, to seek the Kingdom in isolation from a saving
  experience of Christ is a doomed social gospel.
  *'Neglected Themes in Modern Preaching'*

## Excuses

- Jesus' parable of the great feast warns of the dangers of
  procrastination. He describes how the invited guests, 'all
  with one accord, made excuses' – they were busy getting
  married or buying a piece of land or putting a team of
  oxen through their paces – activities on which their
  future security might depend and therefore plausible
  grounds for declining the invitation. But Jesus' point is
  that apart from the Kingdom of God we have no future;
  nothing must take precedence over its claim on us, and if
  we assign to it anything other than the first place in our
  priorities, we are lost.
  *Bible Reflections Round the Christian Year*

## How are we doing?

- When Paul was under house arrest in Rome, he spent his
  last days, according to the final verses of the Acts of the
  Apostles, 'speaking to them urgently of the Kingdom and
  seeking to convince them about Jesus.' The Apostles
  didn't seem to worry overmuch about the Church's
  destiny; the question which preoccupied them was not,
  'How are *we* doing?' – that's a question about statistics,
  but 'What is *he* doing?' – a question about mission; *he*
  being the Holy Spirit who links together the people of
  God not in some formal organisation with a membership

ticket but through his unpredictable, exhilarating presence, which like the wind shows a majestic disregard for official structures.
*Sermon – Wesley's Chapel*

## Old-time religion

- There's a chorus they used to sing in the Methodist chapel where I was brought up that ran:

  *'Give me the old-time religion*
  *It's good enough for me*
  *It was good enough for Moses*
  *And it's good enough for me.'*

  The point is: the old-time religion wasn't good enough for Moses – he looked on his depressed, defrauded and exploited people and cried, 'Let my people go!' and exchanged the old-time religion of comfortable servitude in Egypt for the religion of social revolution in the dangerous wilderness.
  *Sermon – Wesley's Chapel*

## The Messianic Secret

- Considering how majestic is the concept of the Kingdom of God and how deep its roots thrust into the history of the Jews, Jesus' teaching about it seems curiously parochial. What can we learn about it from short stories whose characters are busy housewives, rapacious landlords, efficient servants, crooked managers and the like? All of them act more or less to type, though there is the occasional unexpected twist to the plot. Presumably Jesus is saying that the Messianic Secret is hidden in the concrete actualities of life, its everyday relationships and ordinary tasks. For those with eyes to see, there is something about the specific which reveals the nature of the

universal, something at arm's length that points to the ultimately unreachable.
*Bugles in the Afternoon*

## Fast track

• Jesus said that prostitutes and outcasts enter the Kingdom of Heaven before the righteous because they are too far gone to put on an act; posturing is beyond them. There is a fast track into the Kingdom for the desperate, but it is a long way round for those who wish to play games with God.
*God in the Shower*

## In sum

• Austen Farrer said it best. God set up his divine kingdom in the human neighbourhood, and let things take their course.
*Starting from Scratch*

## LITURGY

## Social rhythms

• The church's liturgical calendar once determined the pattern of our nation's life. Our festivals were Britain's holidays, our Sabbath was Britain's day of rest, our church bells told Britain when to assemble for worship. But changing work patterns, the demands of a consumer society and the increasing mobility of citizens mean that the church's calendar no longer matches the social rhythms of our nation, nor even the religious needs of our citizens of other faiths. Hence, the gulf between ourselves and the rest of society widens ever further – which would

not trouble an exclusive sect content to write off God's world as irredeemably evil, but that is not an option open to the Holy Catholic Church.
*Methodist Recorder*

## Sacred space and time

- People have a deep need for ritual. Ritual is the ceremonial re-enactment of the stories by which we live. By imposing order on an untidy, frightening and unpredictable world, ritual directs human beings into the flow of sacred power in the way iron filings line up in response to magnetic influence. The core of ritual is a crucial event which generates loyalty in those who respond to its recital.
  *Wrestling with an Angel*

## Nonconformist malaise

- I used to be careless in preparing a service, spending hours finding the exact pattern of words to address at the congregation through the sermon whilst taking only a few minutes to put together a few sentences to be directed at God in worship. It was the Nonconformist malaise and I had a bad case of it.
  *The Word and the Words*

## Liturgical exuberance

- Preaching requires a trumpet, liturgy demands a full orchestra. And the full range of human senses may be employed, sight, sound, taste, smell and touch. Music, silence, visual images and tangible objects may all have an honourable place in that work of the people we call liturgy. And of course, bursts of exuberance are in order, provided they are spontaneous; they cannot be contrived.
  *Bugles in the Afternoon*

- One of my complaints about too much modern liturgy is not that it is bad but it is bare, short on style. The language is too flimsy to bear the weight of mystery; it doesn't feed the imagination, it is as thin as workhouse gruel.

  *Bugles in the Afternoon*


## Total exposition

- It is not the sermon alone which proclaims the Gospel. People used to travel very long distances to hear John Henry Newman say the Office, and C. H. Spurgeon's public reading of the Psalms was apparently a never-to-be-forgotten experience. The living word can be heard without any exposition, or rather, it is expounded in our manner, demeanour and voice, our entire bearing as we lead divine worship. The reverence with which Alexander Whyte opened the pulpit Bible to seek out his text, and at the end of the sermon, the decisive crash as he slammed it shut as though he had physically to tear himself away from it; these were not oratorical tricks, they were quite unconscious evidences of the centrality of the Word of God in his life.

  *William Barclay Memorial Lecture*


## Godly gimmickry

- To dispel the stultifying formalism of too much worship, some of us have turned ourselves into sanctified show-men and run the gamut of gimmickry. We have done everything short of standing on our heads in the pulpit and drawing rabbits out of the collection-bag to liven things up. Our motives have been honourable but the results counter-productive. Liturgy is meant to express the rhythm of real life, and it just isn't part of the life-style

of the average Christian to dance down the aisle with a
daffodil behind his ear singing 'Lord of the Dance'.
*Bugles in the Afternoon*


## LOVE

### Elusive

• No word in the English language is more elusive than
love. And when we talk about God's love, its resonances
with our own experience bring it so easily into the context of earthly relationships that God's radical otherness
is compromised. So much so, that though the phrase
'God is love' is of course in the Bible, it is probably
wise to add a qualifier such as 'eternal' or 'redeeming' or
'gracious' love. That was Bishop Ian Ramsey's view.
*Mankind My Church*


### Divine love recognised

• It is not possible to consider any aspect of the Christian
faith, to discuss any Christian doctrine without finding
behind and beyond the particular theme the universal
reality of God's love. What is faith but Divine love recog-
nised? Hope is Divine love's triumph foreshadowed;
revelation is Divine love doing a new thing; conversion is
Divine love given best; salvation is Divine love at peace;
purity is Divine love in dangerous places; silence is Divine
love pondering its next move; Prayer is Divine love
soliloquising. 'God is love' is the subtext of all sermons.
*What the Papers Didn't Say*

## A folk tale

- I once read a Czech folk tale about two neighbours. 'Do you love me?' asked one. 'Deeply,' said the other. 'Do you know what gives me pain?' 'How can I know that?' 'If you do not know that, how can you say you love me?'
*What the Papers Didn't Say*


## Interpreted by love

- God's love encompasses everything – the world, life and death, all things present and to come; there are no moral voids, no profane spaces in the universe. Even when our sin separates us from God, the gulf is filled with his love. As the hymn puts it, even the silence of eternity is 'interpreted by love'.
*Mankind My Church*


## Consider the breadth of God's love

- The breadth of God's love leads us to the conclusion that the problems that face the world are of such proportions that they will require the gifts and skills of all humanity for their solution. Even the recovery of theological power in the Church depends to a great extent upon the willingness of Christians to draw upon theological and spiritual resources to be found beyond their own tradition. We need to explore what it means to be part of God's great ecclesia, not the one stamped on our membership cards but that graven on our souls.
*Mankind My Church*


## Eighty per cent water

- There have been many profiles in the past few days about the newly appointed Archbishop of Canterbury, but I can

reveal exclusively to listeners of the *Today* programme a fact I have not read anywhere else. The Archbishop is made up of eighty per cent water, and the other twenty per cent consists of chemicals you could buy at a pharmacist for a couple of pounds. So is the rest of humanity. What a wonder it is that human beings put together from the contents of a child's chemistry set could have created civilisations, art, literature and music. Most wonderful of all, this chemical cocktail can give and receive love.
*'Thought for the Day' – BBC Radio 4*

## Love and imagination

- What relevance can that bald cliché, God is love, have to the hectic world of politics and international relations? Well, the root of many of society's problems is to be found not in technical political and economic issues but in a lack of trust and mutual respect between its members. It is easy to look at others without actually seeing them. We see a stereotype shaped by our prejudices and ignorance. Love gives us the power of imagination to put ourselves in someone else's shoes and see how our actions look from the other side of the tracks, south of the equator or on the wrong side of the breadline.
  *Things Shaken, Things Unshaken*

## Scale of values

- What do I supremely value? It can't be money because I may lose it, or sex because such appetites wane, or ambition because as the years take their toll once desirable goals recede beyond my reach. I suppose if I were pushed, I would confess, a little coyly: it is when I try to do what is right and stand for the truth as best I can, that the conviction is borne in on me that I'm hitting a sort of bedrock in my life, in some way aligning myself with its

ultimate reality. This, I believe, is the way things are meant to be; qualities such as love, goodness, truth and beauty seem not to be inventions but revelations; they are not what I import into my life but what I find there. These are what I value supremely.
*Start Your Own Religion*


## The worthwhile

- I believe it is through the presence of love, goodness, truth and beauty in my life that I am in touch with ultimate reality, and I sense this isn't just a personal fancy on my part, but the rational order of things. The practical proof of all this is that there is nothing worthwhile I have achieved in which love, truth, beauty and goodness played no part. And when I analyse my moral failures, it is not hard to locate the cause in my unwillingness or incapacity to stand by the loving, the true, the beautiful or the good at some point.
*Start Your Own Religion*


## MINISTRY

## A disembodied bundle of virtue?

- The minister is a human being – a statement the average congregation will receive with the hoots of derision reserved for a fool who told them he had discovered that two and two makes four. Yet good Christians who are well aware that two and two equals four still behave as though a parson were not so much a human being as a disembodied bundle of virtue they pay to be good on their behalf.
*Bugles in the Afternoon*

## The servant as leader

- We sometimes pray that God will raise up another giant of faith such as John Wesley. I know it is gross heresy but I wonder whether too many personalities of the stature of Wesley are even good for the Church. It is said that no grass grew where Emperor Caligula's horse had stood. There is always a danger that more modestly endowed followers may wilt and become passive in the shadow of towering personalities. Though the model of leadership in the Old Testament was the dominant King – and Wesley was certainly monarchical in his manner – according to the New Testament, Jesus introduced a revolutionary concept of leadership, choosing *doulos*, a word that can be used to denote a worker or even a slave. This accords well with the notion of Christianity as the faith of and for the little people of the earth, though this does not exempt them from attempting great things for God.
*Bugles in the Afternoon*


## Not our master

- The minister is truly the servant of the people but they are not his or her master. When Paul was before Agrippa describing his conversion, he claims that on the Damascus Road, God said to him, 'Stand on your feet and I will make you a minister, *delivering you from the people*.' That is something ministers may need, to be delivered from the people who will otherwise smother them with kindness and trap them in a silken web of obligation, so that it seems the basest ingratitude to stand against them with a prophetic word that cuts like a sword through the happy fellowship. The reason why ministers dare stand against the people at all is because at their ordination, when the words are spoken over them, 'Take thou authority to be a minister in the church of God', it is not a list of members but a Bible that is thrust into their hands.

*Ordination sermon*

## Stranger in the midst

- The average minister or priest is a clerical wanderer. He or she serves the people and then moves on elsewhere. There is a parable here. This parsonic wanderer on the face of the earth is a living reminder to the people of God that there may be many things they can do for themselves but they cannot save themselves. Their salvation comes from outside. So when next you're tempted to moan that the newly arrived parson is cutting across established ways of doing things, turn your complaint into a parable and see him or her not as a square peg in a round hole but the alien in your midst who represents that other Outsider waiting to break in with the gift of salvation.

*Bugles in the Afternoon*

## A special case

- The world finds it hard to accept that ministry can be truly exercised through full-blooded and robust personality. During the Second World War, a notice was displayed in Employment Exchanges which ran: 'All persons in the following age-groups are required to register for national service except lunatics, the blind and ministers of religion.' Now, whatever interpretation is placed on that classification, the main point is clear: the government thought the minister to be a special case; he or she has been exempted by heredity or providence from ordinary human characteristics. But the incarnation declares that God's truth does not exist in a vacuum but is expressed through a human life. One moral must surely be that if the minister as messenger can make the Gospel his or her own, anyone can.

*Ordination sermon*


## No immunity

- Ordination is not the spiritual equivalent of that hot wire which used to be drawn across the brain of uncontrollable patients to turn them into happy vegetables. It offers no immunity from the pressures that bear upon every personality; indeed, it adds to them.
*God in the Shower*


## The *theatron*

- Paul writes of Christians making public spectacles of themselves. The Greek word he uses is *theatron* which has echoes of the London Palladium, and it refers to a dumb animal being dragged into the arena to be humiliated for the pleasure of the crowd. Of no one is that truer than of ministers or priests who are bound to fall flat on their faces again and again because by definition they are in a job too big for them; their profession and performance will sometimes be ludicrously at odds, attracting the ridicule of the bald headed man selling hair restorer.
*Wrestling with an Angel*


## Holy tension

- The minister is the servant of a historical Word that refers to unrepeatable events, and it is his or her priestly role to rehearse them within the Church for ever. But this Word is also an Apostolic Word which needs new voices to tell it forth as God's response to the life of a particular time, and this involves the minister as prophet. Priestly obedience is to a holy tradition; prophetic obedience is to

a vision. And the minister contracts to live with this inevitable tension between the two – not the tension between prophets and priests in the ministry, but that of the prophet and priest in every minister.
*Mankind My Church*


## Staking everything

• In the end, ministers stake everything on the truth of the Gospel. If it is true, they have everything; if it is false, they have nothing. That is quite a gamble on which to stake a life-time's work. There is a degree of daring in the ministerial vocation that redeems a life from mediocrity.
*God in the Shower*


## Successor to the Apostles

• I find the traditional understanding of the Apostolic Succession hard to swallow because, with every respect to our Anglican and Catholic friends, I cannot see that the Apostles had any linear descendants. Those who had the unique privilege of personal contact with the historical Jesus took it to the grave with them. If there is any successor to the Apostles it must surely be the New Testament.
*Starting from Scratch*


## Absolute openness

• We live at a time when ministers are required to lay their integrity on the line with absolute openness. They cannot hide behind the skirts of the bishops or the robes of the doctors. They cannot pick other men's flowers or preach other men's sermons or recite other men's beliefs with any hope of carrying conviction. In one sense, ministers have not been sent from God with any message, they are

that message – its weight their weight, its convincing power a direct function of their spiritual and intellectual capacity to open themselves to the Gospel.
*Mankind My Church*

## Priesthood of most believers?

- The name a child is given at baptism symbolises a solemn obligation on the Church's part to support and cherish him or her. The minister too has a name and a soul to be saved. Many a ministerial soul has been put in jeopardy in churches which practise a grotesque parody of Protestantism and believe in the priesthood of all believers except the parson.
  *Mankind My Church*

## MISSION

### The grace to receive

- The question is not: 'Have we the resources to teach others what we know of Christ?', but, 'Have we the grace to receive what he wishes to teach us through Christians who in many languages and a bewildering variety of churchmanship proclaim him as Lord?'
  *Report of the Methodist Overseas Division, 1974*

### What's in a word?

- There is a move to abandon the old term 'missionary' and replace it with another. I can quite see why, but one wonders: is it the word or the reality that is on trial? If it is the word, one must ask what other conveys the same sense of Divine calling, commissioning and dispatch with a writ that runs to the ends of the earth? And surely, an

office hallowed in Christian tradition through being borne by such a glorious company of doctors, saints and martyrs must outlast any arguments about appropriate terminology?
*The End of the Missionary?*


## Having nothing

- In Africa, I saw that one of the reasons Catholic missionary orders such as the White Fathers were so effective is because they were the only white people poor Africans met who had fewer possessions than they had themselves.
*The End of the Missionary?*


## Enabling the gifts of others

- Christian mission is not an investment but an act of grace – lives and resources poured out regardless of return. And its human dimension can be reduced to this: mission is enabling the gifts of others. It is to empower people spiritually, politically and personally.
*Nothing to Defend*


## The missionary church

- A dead church cannot produce live missionaries nor can one that is insular and inward-looking imbue its members with a world vision. But where churches order their life and witness on the conviction that it is at local level that the reality of the Church universal is made manifest; where faith is truly catholic because it is illuminated by the insights and experience of those within the fellowship who represent a variety of cultures and traditions; where there is an agonised awareness that those across the street are as much in need of the Gospel as those across the world – these are truly missionary churches.

*Report of the Methodist Overseas Division, 1977*

## Giving and receiving

• Mutuality is the only credible relationship between British churches and those who have come into being, under God, through our missionary activity. Here we give, there we receive; in this we lead, in that, we are led; now we listen, then we speak.

*Report of the Methodist Overseas Division, 1977*

## Secular dynamic

• The contemporary thrust in mission is predominantly a lay rather than professional enterprise. The vast majority of Christians away from home do not fall into the traditional category of 'missionary'. Most are carried hither and thither across the world by a secular dynamic. The Lord can speak as clearly through a newspaper's International Situations Vacant advert as a missionary society's appeal for recruits.

*Report of the Methodist Overseas Division, 1977*

## Testing the spirits

• We have moved through a period when we swept aside the views of the leaders of younger churches with patronising condescension to one where we assume their infallibility. We feel they must be right now because we were wrong in the past. The Bible says, 'Test the spirits that they are of God.' It does not add, 'unless of course they issue from the developing world in which case it can be taken for granted.'

*Annual Sermon of the Church Missionary Society*

- The new generation of missionaries will be responsible not to those who sent them but to those to whom they are sent.
  *The End of the Missionary?*

- The word became flesh to bind God and his world together in the hearts and minds of believers. God without the world is an enigmatic abstraction; the world without God is a terrifying fiction.
  *Christmas morning sermon*

## Get walking

- This world is an unfinished work which we humans can only make something of as we make something of ourselves. Ask for bread and God doesn't drop a loaf into your lap but sprinkles a few seeds into your hands. Cry for peace and he will grant you the capacity for sacrifice. Yearn for the Promised Land and he will point first to the desert and then at your feet and tell you to get walking.
  *The Hammer of the Lord*

## No copyright on Christ

- There is a great fuss being made in religious circles about the enormous sales of the novel *The Da Vinci Code* which is a fictional account of Jesus marrying Mary Magdalene and ending his days in France. Words like 'blasphemy' are being bandied around. But the author had every right to bring his imagination to bear on the story of Jesus. Christians do not own the copyright on Christ; they freely relinquished that when they declared him to be not just the founder of a Jewish sub-sect but the Lord of all life. He belongs in the public domain, and authors and artists are entitled to portray him to the limits of their imagination, as they have done for two

millennia. Instead of railing against the book, perhaps Christians ought to be asking: why has the Christian imagination withered? If we cannot connect with a popular culture which is obviously interested in religious themes, as *The Da Vinci Code* demonstrates, then belly-aching about those who can will get us nowhere.
*Methodist Recorder*

## Blessing or curse?

- The greatest spiritual challenge the Church now faces is not the opposition or apathy of a secular society but our own sense of the apparent inconclusiveness of the Christian mission. Eighty generations after the Gospel was first heard, Christianity remains scarred by division, bigotry and uncharity; it is still capable of fomenting wars, persecution and intolerance in Christ's name. Of course, that's not the whole story, or even most of it; there are many entries on the credit side of the account. Christianity has raised human beings to a higher spiritual plane, inspired heroic ventures in philosophical and political thought, in music and art, in exploration and discovery, in philanthropy and education. But will a balance sheet which shows that *all things considered*, Christianity has been more of a blessing than a curse, convince the world of the truth of our absolute claims for Christ?
*Millennium sermon*

## Christians A, B and C

- The Christian constituency in the modern world is messy and confused. I divide it into believers A, B and C. Believers A are traditional belongers for whom the service of the church is their life. Besides being the focus of their worship, it is the place where they spend much of their non-working time and a fair slice of their income. There they find friends and often life partners. They would be utterly lost without the church, and it could not function without them. They regard their membership of the church as a total and life-long commitment because for them involvement with organised religion is a Christian vocation.

Believers B are often referred to as lapsed members. For many reasons they have left the Church and have no interest in ecclesiastical maintenance. Cathedral deans report that there has been a marked increase not just in people visiting cathedrals as tourists but as worshippers who wish to slip into the statutory services and then melt back into the world without identifying themselves. The secular world is of interest to Believers B for its own sake and not because it can be turned to some religious purpose. If they discern God's will at all, they see it in the concrete situation; they don't look to the church to mediate it to them. Yet their mind-set has been shaped by the Christian outlook on the world and they often assume the teaching of Jesus as the source of their moral values.

Believers C are those who have never belonged to the church but identify themselves in general with movements and currents of thought that have been wholly or partially religious in origin – various forms of political radicalism, green movements and crusades against poverty, discrimination and war. They are interested in the fundamental issues of religion such as the nature of the transcendent and the meaning of human life. Jesus sharply warned his disciples against discounting such allies – 'I have not found such faith in Israel,' he said when an outsider, a Believer C, showed more spiritual discernment than they had.

These categories cannot be sharply distinguished and there is constant movement between them, but in general, believers B and C are beyond the range of conventional church activities. We may deeply regret that fact but we have a straight choice – either to write them off as lost to Christ and his Kingdom, which is a judgement we dare not make since only Jesus knows his own – or accept their witness for what it is worth and work alongside them.

*The Christian Conundrum – BBC Radio 2*


# MUSIC

## Too deep for words

- From time immemorial, people have celebrated in song and dance the most profound experiences of their lives – life and death, joy and tragedy, communion and loneliness. From the ancient Israelites dancing before the ark of the Lord to mourners in rural Ireland returning from a funeral on a farm cart to the accompaniment of a fiddler playing an Irish jig, humanity has set its deepest hopes and fears to music because music strikes into the psyche to express things too soul-shaking or too ambiguous to render into words. Gustav Mahler confessed that he only began to compose music because he could not put his deepest feelings into words.

  *Wrestling with an Angel*


## Nostalgia

- I left Oxford in the 1950s to go off to be a missionary in Central Africa. On a glorious summer's afternoon, I walked through a leafy Wellington Square on the way to the station to get the train for Southampton and then the Union Castle boat to Cape Town. From an open attic window floated the strains of Vaughan Williams' *Variations on a Theme by Thomas Tallis*. On a number of occasions in the years that followed I found myself in

turbulent, even violent situations, but I only had to hear that theme and I was reminded that life is not all hunger and war and strife, it has gentleness and beauty and peace too. Thus did the Psalmist talk of 'singing the Lord's song in a strange land'.
*St Cecilia's Day sermon*


## Incarnate in song

• During the freedom struggle in Africa, when colonial governments imprisoned nationalist leaders or banned them from addressing meetings, the message of freedom still spread like wildfire because the people incarnated it in popular songs. It was possible to muzzle the orator and disperse the crowd but there was no way of stopping the people from singing. Little wonder that the Scottish patriot Fletcher of Saltoun wrote, 'Let me make a country's songs, then anyone can make its laws.' Words divide us into Yea and Nay Sayers: music unites us.
*Wrestling with an Angel*


## Fulfilment

• Music and religion have this in common. At their centre is rhythm – a pulsating flow which resonates with something utterly fundamental at the very heart of things. To move with this rhythm is to be fulfilled; to get cross-grained to it is to feel alienation and unease – disharmony. A long time ago Confucius noted this affinity between music and religion. He wrote: 'In music of the grandest style, there is the same harmony that prevails between heaven and earth' – a sense of wholeness, of things being as they were intended to be.
*Wrestling with an Angel*

## The congregation strikes back

- In many aspects of religion it is the professional, the priest or minister or clergyman or even the choir-master who rules the roost, by virtue of authority or knowledge or power. But the hymn-book is the place where the congregation strikes back. Here is firm proof of that venerable doctrine, the Priesthood of all Believers. Lay people may not be able to choose the cardinal doctrines of their faith – the charismatic leaders and sacred conclaves do that – but they *can* decide what popular expressions of their faith will prevail. They vote not with their feet but with their voices. Their stubborn insistence on cherishing some hymns and studiously neglecting others decides the shape and content of mass religion. Let the professors of music sniffily declare a tune banal or sentimental; let the theologians loftily pronounce the words doggerel or even heretical, but if the people take that hymn to their hearts, sooner or later it will triumph.
  *'Songs of Praise' anniversary sermon*

- People can sing beyond their conscious beliefs. I recall in the 1960s asking a radical theologian if he could say the Apostles Creed. 'No,' he replied, 'but I can sing it!'
  *'Songs of Praise' anniversary sermon*

## Heavenly music

- The great theologian Karl Barth wrote that when he got to heaven he would expect to hear the music of Bach being played on formal occasions, but when the heavenly host was relaxing it would be to the strains of Mozart.
  *Bible Reflections Round the Christian Year*

## The very first time

- The old faith becomes new when it is heard through fresh voices and alien accents. G. K. Chesterton said, 'You can hear something nine hundred and ninety-nine times and you are quite safe, but if you hear for the thousandth you are in danger of hearing it for the first time.'
  *St Cecilia's Day sermon*

## Spiritual time-bombs

- Hymns plant spiritual time-bombs in the mind. One way or another, often as children, we learn hymns; then as time wears on they slip our memories, secular preoccupations lead us to forget the Lord's song. But deep, deep in our minds, they slumber on, these magic images, and can unaccountably come to life again, triggered by a crisis or the need to celebrate or the desire for comfort – and the detonator is often the tune. Very often all we have to do is hum the tune and the words come back to us. This is the secret of the continuing power of programmes such as *Songs of Praise*.
  *St Cecilia's Day sermon*

## Trumpets and choirs

- The author of the Book of Revelation tries as best he can to paint a picture in words of the new heaven and earth. But when he runs out of vocabulary he brings on the trumpets and choirs. Trumpet blasts announce the abolition of all the terrible scourges that have afflicted humanity, and choirs sing antiphonally of the glory of God.
  *St Cecilia's Day sermon*

## Carolling the faith

- Confront the average person with those sonorous phrases in the Nicene Creed, 'Very God of Very God', 'Begotten not made', 'Being of one substance with the Father', and he or she will say, 'Oh, all that philosophical stuff's beyond me!', but give them Charles Wesley's Christmas carol, 'Hark, the herald angels sing,' and they will bellow away, 'Veiled in flesh the Godhead see, hail the incarnate deity.' That's high theology brought alive to the sound of the trumpet. Or take that glorious phrase, 'Our God, contracted to a span' – radicals and evangelicals, Catholics and liberals all sing it with great gusto at carol services. Yet analyse each word forensically and you'll have the theological schools in uproar. There is the stuff of endless argument in the words, yet the image affirms an incontestable truth.
*God-in-a-Box*


## MYSTERY

### No witnesses

- Both ends of history are shrouded in impenetrable darkness. There were no human eye-witnesses to creation and who can imagine what form the consummation will take? Yet we have much to learn from the old Hebrews who gave us Genesis. As they pondered on the mystery of creation, they resisted the temptation to indulge in pseudo-science; instead they addressed themselves to the grand mystery – the nature of the creator God. They asked, 'How would the God we know *now* have acted *then*?' If the creation speaks of order, love and trust, it is because, despite his mysterious nature, the God in whom they believed had demonstrated trustworthiness and moral consistency. Similarly, there are clues to the way

God will deal with the End by asking the parallel question: how will the God we know now deal with things then?
*God in the Shower*


## Knowledge in a mystery

• The mysterious does not lose its essential depth when elements of it are revealed. In this sense, the Kingdom of God is described in Mark's Gospel as a mystery, and Paul refers to Jesus as the 'Mystery of God'. The more we learn of Christ, the more mysterious his true nature is revealed to be. As John Henry Newman put it, 'A revelation is a religious doctrine viewed on its illuminated side; a mystery is the self-same doctrine from the side unilluminated.'
*'Neglected Themes in Modern Preaching'*


## Inevitable silence

• We have neither words nor images to capture the essence of divine mystery. 'Mystery' – the Greek term means to close one's mouth – for every attempt to speak adequately about it is doomed.
*Let God be God*


## Neither puzzle nor problem

• The word 'mystery' has been corrupted in everyday speech. When people use it, they are usually referring to a crime story. In fact, crime stories are rarely mysteries; they are either puzzles or problems. A puzzle is a faulty way of looking at something and can be solved by altering one's perspective. The fact that ships did not fall off the edge of the earth was a puzzle to those who believed the earth was flat. The puzzle was solved when people

stopped thinking like flat-earthers. A mystery cannot be solved, it can only be explored, and even then inadequately – the more light is cast on it, the greater the area of darkness stretching beyond it.
*Let God be God*


## Mercy in mystery

- Life within history is only possible because God is cloaked in mystery. His unequivocal presence must embody his judgement. Everything hidden would be revealed, a line drawn under all accounts and the human story would come to an end. There is mercy in the mystery of God.
*Let God be God*


## On trying to explain everything

- One reason I am a Christian is that the faith explains more about me and the world I inhabit and explains them better than any other ideologies or systems of ideas I have come across. But it does not make the mistake of trying to explain everything. It retains a proper reticence about the strictly mysterious element in life – not what is as yet unknown until the Big Brains get around to unravelling it, but what will remain for ever unknowable – mystery not to be found beyond the present frontiers of knowledge but existing at the heart of the simplest things and everyday experiences.
*Let God be God*


## Painful point

- As the congregation sang 'The Lord is my shepherd' at a televised service for the thousands of victims of the Indian Ocean tsunami, I heard a sceptical cameraman

mutter, 'Some shepherd!' One can see his point, and many members of the general public would too. The challenge to the Church as the examination papers say is 'Explain.' This is where the mystery of God becomes acutely painful.
*Methodist Recorder*

## Neither to be found nor evaded

• God's mysterious reality tantalises us. He is an elusive Pimpernel whom we seek here, there and everywhere. And yet though God cannot be found, the paradox is that he cannot be evaded either. It is the same God Job is seeking – 'Oh, that I knew where I might find him!' – whom the Psalmist cannot escape, 'Where shall I flee from thy presence?'
*Bible Reflections Round the Christian Year*

## Mystery in the everyday

• There's a fascinating verse in the Book of Proverbs about mystery. 'Four things I do not understand; the way of an eagle in the sky, the way of a serpent on a rock, the way of a ship on the sea and the way of a man with a maid.' Now, we can help out the poor chap who wrote Proverbs – the eagle flies because it displaces air by the lateral movement of its wings. The serpent moves across the rock by the rippling effect of muscles over its ribs; the way of a ship on the sea is not mystery to anyone familiar with exact navigation, and as for the dealings of a man with a maid, a combination of biology and psychology will explain them. But that's what the author of Proverbs meant. He's not talking about aerodynamics but about the grace and freedom of the eagle in motion – mystery; about the serpent's sinuousness which from ancient times has symbolised the power and subtlety of evil – mystery.

Nor is it the laws of navigation that determine the ship's destination but that mysterious human urge for voyaging, for pushing beyond all known frontiers. And as for the man and the maid . . . what else will they find themselves doing but wrestling with the mystery of the other, for the sacrificial and healing power of love cannot be charted by the chromosomes?

*Let God be God*

# NAME

## The power of a name

- In the ancient world, to know a person's name gave one power over him or her. Hence, Moses' demand to know God's name, and his refusal to disclose it. As late as the 19th century, in rural England, when a father chose his baby's name, it was customary for him to conceal it from everyone, even the mother, until he whispered it to the godparents at the baptism. And in traditional African societies to this day, to know someone's name is to have a claim on him. I saw old Zambians pitch up at State House, President Kaunda's official residence, without an appointment, and demand to see him. They knew him by name and that was enough. And the leader, however busy, would try to find time to see them.

*Out of Africa's Crucible*

## Unpronounceable

- Because the original text of the Old Testament had no vowels, the divine name was represented by four consonants, JHWH. The Jews would not utter it and so used Adoni, Lord or Ha Shem, the Name. In fact, JHWH is unpronounceable, whichever vowels are added to it in whatever order. It is not a name we can take in vain. It wasn't an Israelite name, so God avoids any racial or regional identity; he is the God of all the world. Nor is it a name that could be employed in a magic spell: God will not allow himself to be used for an ulterior purpose. This unpronounceable name is also a protection against idolatry.

*The Word and the Words*


## The God everywhere and nowhere

- When the Emperor Ptolemy sacked Jerusalem in AD 63, and entered the Holy of Holies in the Great Temple, he was baffled to find an empty room – no picture, ascription or image. Emptiness is a negative description of the God who cannot be named, described or contained.

*The Word and the Words*


## NONCONFORMITY

## Better blind than deaf

- As a general rule, nonconformists of my childhood years believed it was better to enter the Kingdom of Heaven blind rather than deaf; what the believer saw was marginal to salvation – hence the austerity of the average chapel – whereas what he or she heard was crucial. The chapel was essentially an auditorium for the hearing of the word where acoustics were more important than embellishment. The word was sovereign, given by God, incarnate in Christ, written in the Bible and proclaimed by the preacher, under whom the people sat, as the quaint expression of the time had it.

*Snapshots*

## Following Christ into society

- For nonconformists of my father's generation, any religion however fervent which was taken up with private transactions between the human soul and God was a travesty of all Jesus stood for. It left untouched and unredeemed those structures of society which dehumanised God's children. When Silvester Horne, minister of the City Temple and radical MP, declared in 1911 that his task was not to follow John the Baptist into the wilderness but Christ into society, that image spoke of the social engagement of nonconformity at its best.
*Snapshots*


## PARANORMAL

## The supernatural in Scripture

- As Leslie Weatherhead pointed out, the New Testament is permeated by what would now be called psychic phenomena. It opens with a story about angels, continues with tales of telepathic communication and evil spirits cast out, relates an interview between our Lord and Moses and Elijah who had been dead for centuries, and is crowned by an account of One who rose from the dead, could pass through closed doors, appear and disappear, and who was seen after his death by hundreds of the faithful.
*Methodist Recorder*


## The tearing of the veil

- My father, who served in the trenches in the First World War, occasionally talked, though with great reluctance, about a close comrade who was killed at his side going over the top at the battle of the Somme. A week later, this

friend appeared at the other end of the trench in which my father was sheltering, and beckoned him over. After my father had left the dug-out, a shell landed on it killing a couple of soldiers he had been chatting with. Then his friend disappeared. My father drew no moral from this incident and was little concerned whether anyone believed him or not. He knew what he knew. But if there is such a thing as a veil between this world and the next, then it might be in carnage, violence and turmoil like the First World War that it is torn apart. Well-attested stories of occult happenings during that war fill many volumes.
*Remembrance Day sermon*

## Explaining the paranormal

- There are natural explanations for many so-called paranormal experiences – psychologists talk about imprinted memories, the power of the unconscious or the telepathic powers of mediums, and the physicists have got in on the act by suggesting that Quantum Theory points to the possibility of multiple space–time systems which may occasionally collide. But in trying to nail down a paranormal experience using the tools of secular knowledge, it is possible that the unique and irreplaceable element in it is missed – the presence of the sacred.
*Methodist Recorder*

## Weatherhead's witness

- The great Methodist preacher Leslie Weatherhead spent a life-time investigating paranormal phenomena. His first book, *After Death*, published in 1922, was based on his experiences as a First World War chaplain; his last book, *The Christian Agnostic* (1975) reiterated the same convictions confirmed by endless research. He concluded that when everything questionable to do with psychic

phenomena has been rejected – and he had attended many séances and dismissed most of them as frauds – there still remains some evidence that we inhabit 'a universe full of living presences all round us'. This reinforced his belief that the membrane which separates this life from the next is so fragile that Christians should not be surprised when love, which is the controlling force of the universe, sometimes blasts a way through it, either way.
*Methodist Recorder*

## The near hereafter

- What Biblical evidence is there for the convictions of many Christians that they are conscious of the presence of loved ones who have died, though the intensity of the impression fades over time? There is a clause in the Apostles' Creed we barely notice though the early Church made much of it. The Fathers gave great attention to the question: where was Jesus in the days between his death and resurrection? The Creed says he was in Hades, the world of the departed, where according to the first Letter of Peter (3.18) he preached to the spirits in prison. There was also Jesus' promise to the penitent thief on the cross – 'Today you will be with me in paradise' – a state the commentators suggest is an intermediate condition where souls find rest between death and the Last Judgement – in other words, the near hereafter. Certainly in the period between his death and ascension Jesus was plainly not in heaven – the far hereafter – for as he told his disciples, 'I am not yet ascended to my Father.'
*Methodist Recorder*

## 'The truth is out there!'

- Much as we might like to steer clear of the occult, we live in a society saturated with it. This is supposed to be a

post-religious age, and yet popular literature, films and television are obsessed with the supernatural: 'the truth is out there' runs the motto of the vastly popular TV series *The X Files*. Even mass circulation children's books take the paranormal for granted, and few parents appear to raise any objection, judging by the sales figures of J. K. Rowling and Philip Pullman. And the fastest growing religious movements of our time, the New Age cults, have colonised an eerie world at every level from the heights of the astrological to the depths of Middle Earth. Meanwhile, the churches are firmly agnostic about the afterlife. We declare its reality, but shy away from close investigation of it.
*Methodist Recorder*


## Beyond proof

- This matter of life after death was and still is a vast pyramid of human hopes resting on a single question mark. Of course, lack of proof is in itself never decisive, science would not exist if it were. As the philosopher William James remarked, it only takes one white crow to demolish the belief from experience that all crows are black. A single corroborated, unarguable instance of communication from the dead would settle the issue for ever. Some Christians claim that the resurrection of Jesus furnishes such evidence, though the doctrine of the Incarnation must surely suggest he is a special case. There was, of course, Lazarus of Bethany, whom Jesus raised from the dead. If Lazarus said anything about this experience, there is no record of it, and he vanishes from the Gospel story as though he had never been. In any case, Lazarus was brought back to life; Jesus rose from the dead. They are quite different processes.
*Methodist Recorder*

## Here be Dragons!

- Our society in general has an insatiable curiosity about the occult and will seek explanations and reassurance from any guru who offers it. And given our constant declarations in worship and preaching about realities which are supernatural, we can surely say more than the equivalent of the inscription on the unexplored areas of ancient maps: 'Keep Out. There be Dragons here!' After all, we deal in the supernatural every day – any number of sane believers address God in prayer and insist that they have been heard and answered.
  *Methodist Recorder*


## POWER

### Changing the human heart

- Power is the ability to accomplish purpose, and therefore it is not an absolute but a relative thing. Whether something is powerful or not depends on what you want to do with it. A bulldozer is good at tearing up the earth, but try using it to take the top off an egg! Dynamite is powerful for blasting great rocks; it is powerless to lull a baby to sleep. Paul's description of the cross as the power of God seemed an absurdity in a Roman Empire that gloried in military might. Where the aim was to dominate people, the Roman legions represented great power, but in melting stubborn human hearts, the cross has proved to express the power of God.
  *Starting from Scratch*

### Almighty to save

- The question of God's omnipotence, his almightiness, bristles with philosophical problems, but for those of us

who are not scholars, there is only one thing we need to know about it. God's omnipotence consists in this – he is almighty to save.
*Let God be God*


## Divine limitations

• The totality of the divine personality places limits on God's use of power. He is not power alone but also goodness, truth and love. Because he is goodness, he cannot do evil; because he is love he cannot hate, because he is truth he cannot utter an untruth. God's power is in the sure grip of his personality.
*Let God be God*


## Power and patience

• Colonel Robert Ingersoll was an American atheist who went around the country in the late 19th century lecturing on the impossibility of God. After each of his lectures he would hold up his watch, saying as was his custom, 'God, if there is a God, strike me dead within five minutes!' When the five minutes was up, he would snap his watch shut and stride off the stage. Someone told the great preacher Theodore Parker about it. He retorted, 'Does the gentleman imagine he could exhaust the patience of Almighty God in five minutes?'
*The Hammer of the Lord*


## Power and personality

• The nub of the problem in history is that we seek the power God has without being the personality God is. Technologically we have mastered nuclear weapons, morally we are barely fit to handle bows and arrows. Our world is at the mercy of mighty power in the hands of midget men. The challenge of the Gospel is the regeneration of human personality so that human beings can be trusted with power.

*Church and Challenge in a New Africa*


## PRAYER

### Blasphemous prayer

• We pray for the peace of the world and spend much of our substance on sophisticated weapons of war. What precisely are we asking God to do? We can put our trust in the Bomb, that may be prudent in a worldly sense, or we can trust in God, which is a risky but genuine option. But to distribute trust between God and the Bomb is to ally God to what even the weapon's defenders would call a necessary evil. That is blasphemous prayer.

*A Week in the Life of God*


### Hacking Agag to pieces

• We tend to assume all prayer is addressed to God, but there are times when it consists of someone thrashing out his or her problems and making crucial decisions in the presence of God. Call it prayer as moral conflict. General Gordon of Khartoum was a moral man but he wrestled for years with a strong inner temptation. He whimsically named his sin Agag after the Amalekite king slain by Samson on the orders of God. Several times, Gordon wrote in his diary, 'I had a hard half-hour this morning hacking Agag to pieces before the Lord.' That's prayer as moral conflict.

*Get Through Till Nightfall*

## The purification of desire

- Our desires do not become respectable because we offer them to God in prayer. Prayer is the purification of desire. It is not only pointless but unintelligent to entertain a thousand desires when there are only a few choices.
*A Week in the Life of God*


## Religion demands prayer

- It is a matter of common sense that religion demands prayer. To assert that reality is personal, that God is like a loving Father or even a great King, and do nothing to make contact with him, is to render the claim meaning-less. Ultimate reality may as well be a blind force as a personality if it does not invite and return communica-tion. If personal being does not mean having an urge towards self-disclosure and welcoming it in return, it means nothing.
*Start Your Own Religion*


- The notion that God exists to answer our prayers dies hard. There is the story of the man who left his car un-locked in a dangerous neighbourhood. To his relief when he returned it was still there. He drove to church to say a prayer of thanksgiving. When he came out, his car had gone.
*Start Your Own Religion*


## Spiritual evolution

- The evolution of prayer from terror-ridden begging to the ecstatic adoration of the saint is a remarkable chapter in human history. Like art and music, poetry and philo-sophy, prayer is an expansion of the human conscious-

ness in directions whose tiniest beginnings cannot be detected in any other creature.
*Start Your Own Religion*

## At one with the Godhead

- The supreme dignity of intercessory prayer is that it is the one form of prayer we can share with the Persons of the Godhead – 'The Spirit himself makes intercession for us with groanings that cannot be uttered,' wrote Paul.
  *Church and Challenge in a New Africa*

## Christian politics

- Radical Christians who demand that the Church should be more involved in politics, sometimes ignore the fact that intercessory prayer is the only form of politics which is completely Christian. Because all intercession is offered 'through Jesus Christ our Lord', it is purged of the self-seeking and partiality which vitiate other political activities.
  *Mankind My Church*

## The cost of intercession

- It is a good general rule that other things being equal, God is more likely to use us than anyone else through whom to answer our prayers.
  *'Thought for the Day' – BBC Radio 4*

## Blessing our enemies

- During the Second World War, my mother, who was a woman of strong faith, would insist that our family prayers should end with a prayer for our enemies. This

seemed to me utterly bizarre at a time when as we cowered under the stairs the Luftwaffe above our heads was busy trying to flatten the industrial areas of the North West all round us. Only later did I learn that praying for our enemies is the highest expression of the Christian spirit.
*God in the Shower*

- Prayer gives us the opportunity of getting to know someone we rarely meet. I don't mean God; I mean ourselves.
*Sermon*

## Prayer wheel versus machine gun

- The Chinese government is attempting to stamp out Tibetan Buddhism. It seems an unequal contest between a mighty army and bare-footed monks, but for over two thousand years they've been spinning those prayer wheels. No Marxist regime has yet to last a century.
*What the Papers Didn't Say*

- The point about silent prayer is not the absence of sound but the absence of self.
*The Word and the Words*

## PREACHING

## Public performance

- Countless words have been written about the sacredness of the preaching vocation. But at a more down to earth level, preaching is a performance in the sense that we have to face people, look them steadily in the eye and project ourselves, for as the most famous definition of preaching, that of Phillips Brooks, makes clear,

preaching is truth conveyed through personality. Now, although according to the Old Testament, God once spoke through the jawbone of an ass, the pulpit is no place for mice. A preacher may be humble, modest, even diffident, but never timid. A timid preacher is like a nervous surgeon, sawing tentatively here and there without cutting out the problem.
*Raising the Dead*


## Strictly impossible

- It's not that the task you [trainee preachers] have embarked upon is difficult; it isn't; it's strictly impossible. As an art and craft, preaching will entrance, infuriate, depress and exhilarate you, but if you ever reach the point through vast experience that it becomes a doddle, you have not mastered the art of preaching; pride has mastered you.
*Raising the Dead*


## The air of anticipation

- The preacher's goal must be to engender that air of anticipation which has congregations echoing the first words of the frog in the Garden of Eden: 'Lord! How you made me jump!'
*Bugles in the Afternoon*


## From outside

- The sermon is an art form, and the point about all forms of art is that the listener or viewer or reader can get more out of them than the artist put there in the first place. That's why we often say a work of art is a 'revelation' to us. Indeed, whenever we call something inspired, the very word has a double meaning – that it is not just of

exceptional quality but seems to be imbued with power breathed into it from outside. No preacher who invokes the Holy Spirit on his or her work should be surprised about that.
*Methodist Recorder*

- Occasionally it is clear from the comments of the congregation after a service that they apparently heard a different sermon from the one I thought I'd preached. One can only conclude that the Holy Spirit got through in spite of me.
*Raising the Dead*

## Lay preaching

- The genius of lay preaching is that the man or woman who greets the congregation on Sunday in the name of the Lord hails them in the name of a common humanity every other day of the week in the shops, along the road or at the workbench. You cannot hope to be persuasive in the pulpit if you are surly behind the counter, slippery with cash or uncharitable about your neighbours.
*Snapshots*

## Wave in a bottle

- A written sermon is a lifeless husk. There is about the sermon in essence an immediacy, an urgency, a now-or-neverness no more to be captured in cold print than a sea wave can be trapped in a bottle without being reduced to a pint of salt water.
*Raising the Dead*

## Denying understanding

- The people in the pews don't exist in a vacuum from Sunday to Sunday; they are preoccupied by a thousand and one problems of daily living. They need time to clear their minds of irrelevancies, and during the sermon they have to get their thinking onto the same wavelength as your own – remember, you may have spent many hours wrestling with your theme; they come at it fresh. And systematic thought, the following through of an argument, can be hard work, especially for those whose everyday business is quite different. So don't omit steps in the argument or gallop through complexities out of the mistaken belief that in shortening the sermon you are sparing the congregation grief. All you are doing is denying them understanding.

  *'Letter to Andrea about Prayer'*, *Methodist Recorder*

## What did it do?

- When the great Scottish preacher Dr Thomas Chalmers was congratulated on a wonderful sermon, he replied impatiently, 'Yes, but what did it do?' The sermon is not a verbal stroll round some intellectual and spiritual terrain in order to admire the view; it is an urgent summons to a desired destination.

  *Raising the Dead*

## Boring sermons

- As a general rule, boring sermons are the product of unimaginative personalities. And such dullness of personality is not an affliction of nature like colour blindness or tone deafness. It is the end-result of mental laziness, spiritual lassitude and an unwillingness to take risks with ideas or relationships. In sum, it is a refusal to feed our

imagination on the rich variety of human experience, events and personalities God throws across in our path.
*Raising the Dead*


## Forgetting one's lines

• Whatever their chosen method of reminding themselves of their sermon, whether notes, manuscript or memory, preachers should be prepared to go beyond the limits of strict safety in order to inject urgency into communication. Nowhere in the New Testament does it say one will end up in hell for forgetting one's lines. The only biblical act of forgetting which is not excusable is to forget the one in whom we believe.
*The Word and the Words*


## A simple sum

• Note how often the phrase 'You all know', or its equivalent occurs in the apostolic preaching according to the New Testament. It was not an utterly strange message that burst upon the first century. As Dr Johnson said, 'People more frequently need to be reminded than informed.' The preacher's task is rarely to offer a congregation a theme of startling novelty – indeed, if the intention is to expound a totally strange idea, then the preacher is in the business of founding a new religion. The task is more difficult – to give new life and urgency to what is in danger of becoming hackneyed and stale. But it is as well to remember what Socrates said when he was accused of repeating himself: 'If I am asked what two and two make, what can I answer but four?'
*Raising the Dead*

• At all costs, preachers must not make great things small, holy things common or costly things cheap.
*Lecture – College of Preachers*

## Keep the operation short!

- Some modern preaching theorists operate on the principle that the shorter the sermon the better. Call me an ecclesiastical dinosaur but I feel cheated when I sit in the pew and I am treated to a very short sermon. I've come to church with matters of some moment on my mind and conscience and I'm eager to know what God's word has to offer me by way of judgment and renewal. I don't believe he speaks in the pulpit-equivalent of Christmas cracker mottos. If I had to have an operation, I doubt I would say to the surgeon, 'Only one thing matters, keep the operation short!'
*The Word and the Words*

## Don't underestimate

- I fully concede there are times when had I put twice as much effort into the preparation of a sermon I could have said it all in half the time. We mustn't trespass on the congregation's patience, but we mustn't underestimate their purposefulness either. The days have long gone when people went to church because it was the done thing; we may assume our hearers are there because they mean business.
*Lecture – College of Preachers*

## On being oneself

- There is an art gallery in Rome which houses a collection of busts of the Roman Emperors, from the earliest to the last, each one done by a sculptor who was a contemporary of the particular Caesar portrayed. It is possible to trace the decay of a great art from the magnificent Greek marbles of the earliest emperors to the crude representations, little more than wooden dolls, of their Gothic successors. The explanation is simple. The later sculptors

were so overawed by their giant predecessors that they slavishly copied their style rather than modelled from the living subject. What goes for sculpture applies also to preaching. Slavish imitation of our betters saps the springs of our creativity; a genuine if modest original is better than a large-scale counterfeit. It is a mistake to imagine that God prefers the echo of someone's eloquent Te Deum to our own paltry praise.
*Raising the Dead*


## Only originals

- One of the old rabbis said that God never does the same thing twice. We ought never to obliterate our individuality as preachers. It's the only truly original gift we have to offer – everything else to do with preaching has been said and done a million times before in Christian history. God doesn't work through carbon copies; only originals. I suspect that when I have to give an account of my life, God won't say, 'Why weren't you Reinhold Niebuhr or Leslie Weatherhead or George Macleod?' He'll say, 'Why weren't you Colin Morris?'
  *Raising the Dead*


## Topical preaching

- Some preachers who will modestly confess they haven't the foggiest notion what's going on in the head of their pet budgerigar are serenely confident they know what God thinks of the US President, the Middle East situation or the future of nuclear energy.
  *Let God be God*

## The preacher and the Church

- The Church and the preacher's need of each other are mutual. Through the preacher, the Church becomes conscious of itself. In the Church, the preacher draws upon a fount of living faith immeasurably greater than his or her own. The preacher acts upon the Church in order that the Church may act upon the world. Indeed, *as preachers*, we have no access to the world except through the Church, certainly not as a substitute for it.
*William Barclay Memorial Lecture*

## Dynamic relationship

- The relationship between the preacher and congregation is dynamic. The preacher establishes a rhythm which the congregation respond to and amplify in the way one instrument can set off vibrations in others. Their imperceptible drawing-in of breath when a thought grips them; the throat-clearing and restlessness when they've got the point and want to move on; that uneasy silence which falls when they have to grapple with an uncongenial idea – then, like the Athenians to whom Paul spoke of the resurrection, they are signalling, 'We will hear you again on this subject.'
*William Barclay Memorial Lecture*

- A sermon in any other form than spoken speech is like unplayed music.
*The Word and the Words*

## Heard it before?

- Provided it is not laziness which impels you to do it, don't be embarrassed to repeat a sermon. The second time round the congregation will probably be able to quarry fresh treasure out of the same vein of truth. Indeed, any sermon in which a preacher has invested honest effort ought to be heard again. Beethoven didn't compose his Sonatas to be played once. We are not in that league, but any painstakingly crafted sermon is still a creative act, a minor work of art. And though you may deliver the same sermon to the same congregation, something in your life and theirs will have changed since the last time you preached the sermon, and this will give fresh currency to your words.

*Raising the Dead*

## A means to a greater end

• To classify preaching as one of the arts is in no way to belittle or vulgarise it. Considered solely in human terms, preaching is high art. It is a vocation doubly vindicated by both a divine call and human achievement. Yet there is one way that preaching does not conform to the rules of art, or rather transcends them for a greater purpose. In its classical definition, all true art is an end in itself, standing on its own as an enriching experience. In general, beauty is its own justification, and there are forms of oratory where elegance of language, purity of voice and grace of gesture excite our admiration even though we find the orator's theme uncongenial or even repugnant. But a sermon can never be an end in itself, merely a means to a greater end. It is a tool and not an ornament, and to judge it by the canons of artistic appreciation alone is to behave like the tribe who were so overawed by electricity that they began to worship the portable generator as God and power cables as his angels. Art for its own sake may be a splendid cultural ideal but it is not one we preachers can share.

*Raising the Dead*

## Shattering complacency

- It is strange that we clergy, even though we have the clear warning of our Lord, 'Marvel not that the world hate you', manage to persuade ourselves that we shall be failing in Christian charity if our words and actions cause dissension amongst our people and bring upon us the wrath of the community. Yet, how can we hope to confront people with the painful demands of our Lord without shattering their complacency, challenging their attitudes and probing the raw nerve of their besetting sins? I was not just upset but outraged that many of my congregation took against me in Central Africa. Obviously, I preferred to be loved than to be right.
  *The Hour After Midnight*


## PROPHECY

## Forth-telling not foretelling

- We do not assign greatness to a Jeremiah and an Isaiah because we can read into their words forecasts of the great events of our time. They occasionally proved mistaken in their predictions, but they did something much more impressive than mere soothsaying. They traced those forces operating in the human heart and society which in every time will create and destroy great powers and elevate the misuse of human knowledge to the level of the demonic. They addressed their own age and yet spoke to the total human condition.
  *Things Shaken, Things Unshaken*


## Not behind closed doors

- Priests by nature and training tend to be guardians of holy things and sacred places, of correctly performed

rituals and cherished traditions. Prophets, on the other hand, are committed to a public ministry. Whilst the priest whispers in the sanctuary, the prophet bellows in the market place. Christ was not sacrificed on some ritual temple altar in holy silence but as the Letter to the Hebrews said, he was crucified outside the city gate on a public holiday. As Paul pointed out to King Agrippa, our salvation was not accomplished behind closed doors.
*Wrestling with an Angel*

## A traditional ministry

- The biblical prophets were not in the business of founding a new religion but of calling people back to the primitive purity of the old one. They were never theologically fancy-free, plucking diverting notions about God out of thin air and hoping to start a fashion. They were not iconoclasts who like Cromwell's soldiers rampaged through the monasteries having a thoroughly enjoyable time smashing sacred things. When they parted company from their fellow believers it was with deep regret, not adolescent glee. In the same way, their passionate impatience was an expression of slowly maturing conviction and not momentary irritation. They were angry men, not bad tempered ones.
*Wrestling with an Angel*

## Paid to prophesy?

- With the exception of Ezekiel, the Old Testament prophets were laymen. You could argue that prophecy is likely to be a lay vocation for a very practical, even mercenary reason. It sits ill with the clergy to thunder from the pulpit on Sundays about the evils of the acquisitive society and then the next day go into negotiation about stipend increases. Nor is it easy to call down

the judgment of God on organised religion's smugness, inertia and worldliness whilst being paid to organise it. The hand raised one day in prophetic anathema against the religious institution must be stretched out the next day to receive its dole.
*Mankind My Church*


## Prophetic community

• The Hebrew prophets were indomitably solitary, almost self-entire in their convictions, conscious of answering only to God himself for their words. By contrast, the prophetic ministry from New Testament times onwards has been exercised within a framework of corporate discipline. The wry wish of Moses, 'Would that all the Lord's people were prophets!' was granted a long time later at Pentecost where 'all present were filled with the Spirit and began to speak'. From that time, prophecy ceases to be the monopoly of an elite and becomes an essential dimension in the witness of every Christian.
*Pentecost sermon*


## Seeing things whole

• There *are* men and women in the modern church, and outside it, who self-evidently share the same vocation as those Hebrew wild men of the Old Testament. They see things steadily and see them whole, whilst the rest of us thrash around treating the world like a cheap watch – to be subjected to inexpert investigation until all the pieces lie in front of us defying our effort to put them together again.
*Wrestling with an Angel*

### Immovable rocks and feather dusters

- The Prophets were not always on the winning side. It is central to our Faith that God wills to give enduring historic significance to the offering of the widow's mite, the faith which is of a grain of mustard seed. It is a matter of Christian experience that there are some great, immovable rocks which God will not shatter with his sledge hammer until we have attacked them futilely with our feather duster. When we have exhausted all our potentialities we have but reached the fringe of the things which are possible with God.
*The Hour After Midnight*


## SACRAMENTS

### Divine wager

- When we make our communion, all kinds of profound truths are expressed in that historic rite, but one above all – as the bread is placed into our hands, it is as though God is putting himself into our keeping, holding nothing back. It is the ultimate divine wager, that we will not let him down.
*Christmas Day sermon*

- There are two sacraments common to all the great religions. One is the created order, the other is the saint.
*A Week in the Life of God*

- The sacraments compensate for a preacher's weaknesses and vanities. At least, Christ will still be preached at the communion table or font when we have finished spreading confusion in the pulpit.
*The Word and the Words*

## Baptism

- Baptism is a proclamation to the Church and through the Church to the world that all human beings live and move and have their being in God. This is not a privilege they acquire through baptism; the Church baptises them because they have it.
  *The Word and the Words*


## Reaffirmation

- Baptism is something that happens to the child but it is *done* by the Church. The baptism of an infant is a reaffirmation of the baptism of every member present. In a sense, each one relives consciously as adults what they were put through unconsciously as infants.
  *God-in-a-Box*


## Taking away our breath

- The sacramental life of the Church is an attack on the Gnostic mind, the modern flight into abstraction and romantic dreaming. Christianity is about flesh being lacerated and blood spilt, about the weight of hands laid upon us and water stinging the skin and taking away our breath as we plunge beneath the healing stream.
  *God-in-a-Box*


## Power of the Holy

- These signs we call the sacraments say to us that the power of the Holy is available to us not by way of magical rites but through the natural channels along which our energy flows for daily living; profound truths mediated through everyday deeds – taking, breaking, eating, drinking, washing and spilling.
  *Start Your Own Religion*

## Blood thicker than water?

• We say that blood is thicker than water; but this is not so in the Church. It is water, the water of baptism, which is thicker than blood, binding us together as members one of another in a fellowship that goes beyond natural ties.
*'Thought for the Day'* – BBC Radio 4

## SACRIFICE

### An initiative not an acceptance

• Sacrifice must be distinguished from the heroic acceptance of the inevitable. The human quality is the same, but the motive is different. Sacrifice is always active, never passive. It seeks to introduce a new element into a hopeless situation. It is an initiative and never a mere acceptance.
*Mankind My Church*

### A simple but costly solution

• Sacrifice sometimes produces a simple but costly solution to a complex problem. Thus, Captain Oates, Scott's colleague, badly frost-bitten as they struggled to get back to safety from the South Pole, became an intolerable burden on those trying to carry him, yet it was unthinkable that they should abandon him. Oates took the issue out of their hands. He walked out into the night to his death – a simple but costly solution to a complex problem.
*Mankind My Church*

## The supreme sacrifice

- What is the ultimate sacrifice? Everything we possess, including life itself, is a gift from God, and therefore, any sacrifice can be seen as merely returning what has been borrowed to its rightful owner. There is one exception over which we have absolute right of disposal – the human will. By his own choice, God's sovereignty stops short at that point. Hence, the Psalmist described the supreme sacrifice as 'a broken and contrite spirit'.
  *Mankind My Church*

## Not memory but presence

- Sacrifice is not always a choice between the bad and the good; it can be the sacrifice of the good for the better. Jesus exchanged the good life, of teaching, healing and service, for the better – an act of obedience so absolute that it changed the course of history. It transformed him from a fond memory to a living presence and a lively hope.
  *Mankind My Church*

## SAINTS

## Proof positive

- The word 'saint' conjures up visions of pale aesthetes gliding three feet off the ground, exuding clouds of super-heated piety, a lily in one hand and a copy of *Fox's Martyrs* in the other. In fact, they have been an amazing variety of human types, though with certain things in common regardless of the religious labels they wear. Saints are practical proof that a religion works. They claim to speak about ultimate reality from observation and experience rather than from theory or speculation.
  *Start Your Own Religion*

## Radical change

- For saints, religion means the release of love and creative energy that comes from sharing however imperfectly the life of God, and it produces radical change, both in personal character and in the life of society.
  *Start Your Own Religion*

## The Isness of God

- Not all saints have been paragons of conventional virtue. The records show that some were quirky, irascible, difficult to live or work with and often without understanding of the human frailties of ordinary believers. Their imperfections were plain for anyone to see, but whilst dispassionate observers might doubt many things about them, one thing was beyond argument – their utter conviction that when they prayed a real Someone answered them and when they listened a real Someone addressed them. They are guarantors of God's existence. In the words of Baron Von Hugel, saints testify to the Isness of God rather than the Oughtness of morality.
  *Start Your Own Religion*

## Agents of hope

- Saints are agents of hope. They expect everything from their God but nothing from others, and therefore they are neither surprised nor disappointed when their initiatives are rejected and they attract hatred or indifference. Their strategies are dictated neither by prudence nor the demands of strict justice. For them nothing is at stake, whether pride or life itself. Louis Pasteur, the discoverer of vaccination, said that fortune favours the prepared mind; the saint insists that the future favours the gracious spirit. They are the leaven of history, rarely transforming it by dramatic upheaval but by countless imperceptible

but significant demonstrations of the grace of God in action.
*Start Your Own Religion*


## Holy wisdom

- There is appreciation of the saintly character right across the spectrum of religions. Christians venerated the Jew, Martin Buber; Buddhists made pilgrimage to sit at the feet of the Hindu Swami Sri Aurobindo; Gandhi's soulmate was Anglican missionary C. F. Andrewes, whilst Martin Luther King saw Gandhi as his great guiding light; the Hindu Rabindranath Tagore's wisdom was treasured by Christian scholars and Muslim Arabs revered the White Father Charles Foucauld. And Mother Teresa moved with universal acceptance amongst the people of many faiths. The turning circle of sanctity whirls on. Holy wisdom knows no confessional boundaries.
*Start Your Own Religion*


## SCIENCE

### On doing anything

- The spirit of the scientific age is well expressed through the determination that if we humans wish to do *anything* badly enough, assuming it isn't inherently absurd, sooner or later we'll find a way of doing it. Yet this manic drive to push back the frontiers of the possible is in danger of becoming a kind of scientific fatalism; if we *can* do it, we've *got* to do it. Thus the talk now is of exploring the near reaches of the universe. But the critical moral as opposed to scientific question is not, 'Can we put someone on Mars?' but 'Can we *not* put someone on Mars?'

and instead use those resources and skills to better the lot of millions here on earth who have barely the where-withal to live? If we can show such restraint, history may remember us not for our cleverness but for a rarer quality, our humility.
*God in the Shower*


## Parascience

- Christians engage in a paranormal activity every week when they gather in groups to keep rendezvous with a Jew who they believe rose from the dead to transform the quality of their lives. Sceptics call it subjectivism, but by my reckoning when millions of people have the same subjective experience at the same time it is getting near to becoming an objective fact.
*Start Your Own Religion*


## The probability of miracles

- There is a mysterious element in life, call it the super-natural or the spiritual, which penetrates the natural world, and where the two intersect strange things happen. They might just rate as miracles if they reveal something of God's nature as love, for we know the extraordinary things of which even human love is cap-able. I recall an African woman whose child had been pinned down by a fallen tree. She raised it with her bare hands far enough to free her daughter. Engineers said it was impossible. Since divine love is the most powerful force in the universe, it would be amazing if from time to time there weren't miracles, explosions of divine grace that burst through all known barriers to do amazing things we can't explain.
'Thought for the Day' – BBC Radio 4

## Unearned benefits

- The world isn't a clockwork orange in which cause and effect are precisely related. It is a wild thing of beauty and terror, horror and pity, poetry and fire. It doesn't operate according to the law of exact moral transactions so that good is always rewarded by happiness and evil by disaster. As a result we get benefits we haven't earned and suffering we don't deserve.
  *What the Papers Didn't Say*

## A brick with our name on it

- In his Letter to Timothy, Paul talks about 'laying a good foundation for the future'. How do we do that? By standing for causes which are unlikely to achieve fulfilment until long after we are gone. It is no trivial immortality to be able to claim that we stood for the Kingdom in the day of small things. We did the truth, lived by love, refused to give up hope and so created the raw material of a decent future. That is how the most ordinary life can achieve significance, and the bonus is the assurance that in the final edifice of things – that new heaven and new earth – there will be one small brick with our name on it.
  *Out of Africa's Crucible*

## Poetry or science

- It is tragic when scientists lose the sense of the poetry of things. They say, for example, that the sun rises because of the rotation of the earth. Nonsense! The sun rises because God says to it, 'Come on then, get up!' The fact that stars twinkle has nothing to do with their gaseous nature. The stars twinkle because God tells them, 'For my sake, smile!'
  *A Week in the Life of God*

# SILENCE

## Silent witness

- I once heard a German Christian describing how she was at a bus stop in 1937 when the Gestapo came along and took a Jew out of the queue behind her and made him stand on his own. Someone asked, 'What did you do?' She replied, 'I didn't know what to do, so I just went and stood by him silently.' You could preach a dozen sermons against anti-Semitism and not reach that level of eloquence.
  *Let God be God*

## The silence of approval

- I once saw this notice on the skid pad of an advanced driving school: 'Advance confidently unless the hooter sounds a warning that you have made an error.' This is an adult variant of the advice given to young footballers, 'Play to the whistle!' God allows us to grow without constant nagging because he wants the zest of living to be in discovery, the romance in the quest, the flavour of life to be in its surprises. His silence is a benediction on our struggles to achieve maturity; a Divine vote of confidence in our humanity.
  *Let God be God*

## Saying nothing

- The Curé of Ars noticed a peasant farmer frequently kneel in church for long periods without the slightest movement of his lips. 'What do you say to our Lord in your prayers?' the Curé asked. The peasant replied, pointing to the crucifix, 'I say nothing. I look at him and he looks at me.'
  *Sermon – Wesley's Chapel*

## The sounds of silence

- One reason many preachers aren't good at handling silence is that when we stop prating we hear ourselves; all the groanings of our inner dis-ease, like the ominous creaking of a ship's bulkheads in a storm – grinding teeth, tapping fingers, the twanging of stretched nerves. We are not at peace so we drown our inner dissonance under a torrent of words. A preacher's ability to handle silence is an indicator of his or her spiritual condition. The Psalmist's words are both an affirmation and a warning, 'For God alone my soul waits in silence.'
  *The Word and the Words*

## The pause

- All great artists are masters at speaking through silence: the object left out of the picture just where you'd expect it to be; the void in architecture; the caesura, the pause in the middle of a line of verse. Recall, for example, those four thundering Hallelujahs in the 'Hallelujah Chorus'; three of them and then a pause that seems to go on for ever, and then the crashing fourth. And in the throbbing silence is an unspoken 'Hallelujah' as piercing as any of the others.
  *Let God be God*

## The only word

- Jesus did not nag anyone into the Kingdom of Heaven. During his most powerful message, on Calvary, where the redemption of the world was accomplished, he spoke just seven words, and according to the Book of Revelation, even heaven fell silent. It was almost as though the universe held its breath to see whether this deed would be done. St John of the Cross said that throughout the whole of eternity God spoke only one word and that word was Jesus, his Son.

*Bible Reflections Round the Christian Year*

## TERRORISM

### A term of abuse

- In some quarters, the word 'theology' has become almost a term of abuse. When commentators regard something as rarefied, remote from the real world, purely theoretical, they say, 'Let's not get into the theology of all this, let's stick to the point!' Well, the London suicide bombings prove that theology is the point; it is impossible to understand what was going on in the bombers' minds without it.

*Things Shaken, Things Unshaken*

### Sacred explosion

- Suicide bombers are not merely prepared to die in order to strike at the enemy, they want to die, to embrace death eagerly; they cannot wait to enter another world beyond the grave. An astonished police officer, having watched the four London suicide bombers at King's Cross station just moments before they went their separate ways to die and kill on different tube trains, said they were laughing and joking as though going on holiday. They believed they would enter paradise directly by an act of martyrdom, and since they could nominate those who when they died would join them in paradise, their relatives would not grieve for them but celebrate, calling the act itself a 'sacred explosion'.

*Things Shaken, Things Unshaken*

## Seven devils

- There was something demonic about the way Saddam Hussein treated sections of his own people and the neighbours in Iran with whom he went to war. But Jesus told a story about a room occupied by a single devil which the householder swept clean, whereupon seven other devils rushed in to fill the vacuum, 'and the last state was worse than the first'. That is an arguable verdict on the Iraq war. One devil was removed together with every vestige of his regime which included the police, civil service and armed forces. And into the resulting vacuum have poured the devils of internal tribalism and insurgency from other parts of the Middle East. And perhaps the seventh devil is to be found in the small but growing number of our own Muslim citizens whose anger is turning homicidal.
  *'Thought for the Day'* – *BBC Radio 4*


## Big and little laws

- G. K. Chesterton once wrote, 'When you break a big law, you don't get freedom; you don't get anarchy, you get a lot of little laws.' Whether or not we did break a big law by going into Iraq is a matter hotly disputed by the lawyers, and as the Prime Minister has said, history will be the judge of that. But one thing's for sure, we've certainly been lumbered with an awful lot of little laws, over three thousand new statutory instruments, many of them dealing with terrorism. Without doubt, there are measures on that list which are necessary for the safety and security of the realm, and it would be irresponsible not to recognise the fact. But that still leaves the little laws, some of which worry citizens like me. Not being the stuff of which martyrs are made, I would probably obey such laws but I wouldn't respect them. And that's not good for me, nor for democracy. To respect a law means not just obeying it to the letter but affirming the logic and morality underlying it.

*'Thought for the Day'* – *BBC Radio 4*


## The vision of justice, peace and joy

- For the Christian, respect for the law is rooted in the theology of the State. The Apostle Paul told his followers who were having a tough time with the Roman authorities that they must not only obey the law but also recognise that their rulers were God's agents. But he was talking about the big laws that hold a state together against the threat of anarchy; he sat lightly to a lot of little laws, which is why he was always in such trouble. And his ultimate loyalty wasn't to any earthly body of law at all. 'I was not disobedient to the heavenly vision' – the vision of a kingdom of justice, peace and joy for which Jesus lived, died and rose again. For the Christian, this is the bench mark against which all human laws, big or little, must be judged.

*'Thought for the Day'* – *BBC Radio 4*


## Prisoners of conscience

- Potentially, all Christians are prisoners of conscience. Their earthly allegiance is uncertain, their patriotism conditional. They have only one absolute loyalty, stated by Peter when hauled before the authorities in Jerusalem: 'We must obey God rather than man.' This is not to reject the duties of citizenship, just fair warning that if the crunch comes, the conscience of the Christian is, as Luther put it, 'captive to the word of God' rather than the diktat of the state.

*Church and Challenge in a New Africa*

## Good out of evil

- There is a subterranean theme in history the secular historian knows nothing about, but which the Christian must try to uncover as events transpire. The God who chose to tame a pagan king, Cyrus, can bring good out of evil and use the most unlikely of people and institutions for his glory.
  *'Thought for the Day'* – *BBC Radio 4*

## Agents and instruments

- When God chooses to act in history, he uses two forces, his agents and his instruments. His agents are those who respond to his call, prepared to seek first his kingdom. On the other hand, his instruments have no choice, they might be anyone his eyes light upon, who happen to be in the right place at the right time. When their wisdom fails, their foolishness serves him. This is the lesson of the cross, God bending and moulding the most dreadful eventualities to be the instruments of his purpose.
  *'Thought for the Day'* – *BBC Radio 4*

## A sense of proportion

- C. S. Lewis was once asked how he would react in the few seconds between a nuclear weapon being dropped above his head and its detonation. He said, 'I'd think to myself, "You're only a hydrogen bomb; I'm an immortal soul."' Simplistic, some people might think, but if that's what you really believe, you're not going to be panicked very easily by Government warnings about terrorism.
  *'Thought for the Day'* – *BBC Radio 4*

## God on our side?

- We find it hard to accept that God has neither favourites nor enemies. He is not the enemy of our enemies; he is not even the enemy of his enemies. He will not allow himself to be used, recruited to our colours and borne like the ark of the covenant into battle on our side or any other for that matter. All nations including our own tend to develop a monstrous egotism and invite idolatry.
  *Remembrance Day sermon*


## No abstraction

- We talk about a war on terrorism, but 'terrorism' is an abstraction. It was not 'terrorism' in general but a specific group of human beings who killed fifty people in the London tube bombings. We can consign them to a sub-category of humanity – 'Animals!' screamed one tabloid, as though any animal would behave in such a manner – but Christ's command to love our enemies forces us to think of them always as human beings, however evil their actions. And then some people say Christianity is an easy option! What could be harder at the present time than having to believe that just as nothing we humans can do, however virtuous, will make God love us more, so there is nothing we can do, however wicked, that will make God love us less?
  *Things Shaken, Things Unshaken*

- Our love for God is measured by how much we love those we love least in this world.
  *'Thought for the Day' – BBC Radio 4*

## Moderate Christianity

- It is dangerous to pigeon-hole Muslims as either moderates or extremists and then assume these labels determine their attitudes to terrorism. Many Muslims regarded as moderates are utterly militant in their opposition to the Iraq war and desperately exercised at the death of thousands of their co-religionists in the Middle East. On the other hand, Muslims regarded by the authorities as extremists may be ranting preachers calling down fire and brimstone on a decadent West, but it cannot be taken for granted that they would support suicide bombing. After all, ask yourself, what does it mean to be 'moderately' Christian, and how many would want to claim the title?
*'Thought for the Day' – BBC Radio 4*


## Shadow of the Cross

- There is a fundamental tension between the Kingdoms of Caesar and Christ. Yet Calvary was situated in Caesar's territory. A cruciform shadow falls across all the state's activities, not just as a stark symbol of God's judgement, but also as a reminder that the way of the Cross offers redemptive possibilities in the political realm through those who practise sacrifice, forgiveness and mercy.
*Bugles in the Afternoon*


## Sparrow falling to the ground

- There is a heated debate raging about the Government's plan to extend detention without trial to ninety days. They argue that in order to safeguard the majority of citizens, they must take measures which regrettably may bear down unfairly on a minority. But Christianity comes at the issue from the other end; concern not for the many

189

but for the few, for the one, even, who is invisible, ignored, forgotten. As Jesus puts it, God cares for the sparrow that falls unnoticed to the ground. So we must ask not, 'What will the overall effect of this measure be in the war against terrorism?' but, 'How much extra suffering will be caused to one innocent person caught in the net and his family?' And we must ask that question quite simply because Jesus said in so many words that what we do to the prisoner we do to him. There's no way round that one.

*'Thought for the Day' – BBC Radio 4*

## By God's grace

- The shocking particularity of God's love mocks the sweeping judgements we make about both our friends and our enemies; it brings into sharp focus those who are normally invisible, who suffer unnoticed. Jesus is at dinner with a respectable citizen when a prostitute bursts in to pay her respects. His host is outraged, but Jesus says, 'Do you see this woman?' He's not doubting his friend's eyesight. He means, 'Do you see her as she really is, a human being, but also what by God's grace she might still become?'

*Things Shaken, Things Unshaken*

## TRUTH

### Instinctive wisdom

- Truth is the capacity to bring one's thinking and feeling into agreement with the world outside; to value whatever comes our way at its proper worth. Truth usually presents itself to us practically as common sense, that instinctive wisdom based not only on our own experience

but on the accumulated experience of humanity at large. From time immemorial it has kept us in touch with reality – 'pull the other one!' we say when asked to swallow the bizarre or plainly nonsensical.
*Things Shaken, Things Unshaken*


## Strange truth

- We say, 'Truth is stranger than fiction.' But, of course. Fiction is the product of a human mind which will work overtime to make it understandable and believable to other human minds. Indeed, we judge fiction by the extent to which it is believable. Truth is a different matter. Because its source is outside ourselves we must accept it in whatever form it presents itself or else turn it into fiction to make it more digestible. This is what we sometimes do with the Gospel. Whenever we come across a strange truth, we are tempted to bend it a little, trim it at the edges, paraphrase it judiciously to make it more believable. Our motives are entirely honourable but the effect of turning enigmatic truth into a palatable half-truth is to rob the Gospel of its transcendent quality.
*Bugles in the Afternoon*


## Doing the truth

- The Bible treats truth in a special way; to answer the question: How can we become free? The answer is truth of a special kind, saving knowledge – 'You will know the truth and the truth will set you free.' Truth is a stream of life centred on Jesus Christ. There is a daring verb in John's Gospel: 'Those who *do* what is true come to the light.' It means participation in the very being of the one who is the truth.
*Church and Challenge in a New Africa*

### Indefinite benefit

- Truth offers us permanent enrichment of our lives – a fund of spiritual wealth which is not governed by the laws of the natural world whereby one person's gain is another's loss. Truth is capable of indefinite increase, we have an entire universe both within us and outside to explore.
*Start Your Own Religion*

## ZAMBIA

### Living by hope

- I recall visiting Kenneth Kaunda in 1959 when he was in gaol. Squatting on the ground outside his cell, he was busy writing. He showed me page after page of diagrams. They were, he said, the structures of the various levels of government he intended to create when Northern Rhodesia became an independent Zambia. Most Europeans in the territory would have dismissed him as a crazy fantasist – Africans had no vote, few civil rights and only a tiny minority had schooling beyond the most elementary level. Yet a mere five years later, President Kaunda sat in the Governor's old residence, State House, drawing up the legislation which would give effect to the system of government set out in those crude drawings. Africans have a capacity we westerners have lost for living expectantly in the present as though the future were already here.
*Snapshots*

## The unnaturally good

- The new Zambia, like any other nation, is unlikely to
  have an adequate supply of naturally good people on
  whom it can draw in those spheres of public life which
  demand dedication and selflessness. This surely is where
  the Gospel comes in. Though the prime motive of evangelism is not to create a supply of good people who will
  be humanely useful, it is one of the consequences. We call
  them saints, and they are good for the nation's morale.
  The early Church Father, Tertullian, wrote, 'Christian
  saints are hilarious.' At the very least they ought to make
  the lot of their fellow-workers a little more bearable.
  *Church and Challenge in a New Africa*

## An end and a beginning

- At midnight on the 23rd October 1964, Kenneth Kaunda,
  African minister's son, and Sir Evelyn Hone, Governor of
  Northern Rhodesia, stood under the arc lights of the
  Independence Stadium outside the capital. The British
  national anthem was played for the last time, the Union
  Jack was lowered and the new Zambian national anthem
  was played. The tune was an old South African anthem,
  *Nkosi Sikelel Africa*, composed in 1897 by a Methodist
  teacher, Enoch Sontongo. Then the Anglican Archbishop
  of Central Africa, the Roman Catholic Archbishop of
  Lusaka and myself as President of the United Church of
  Zambia had the once in a life-time privilege of saying
  the prayers of dedication that brought the Republic of
  Zambia into existence. The long battle for freedom was
  over; the struggle for mature nationhood was about to
  begin.
  *Mankind My Church*

# Sources and Acknowledgements

Books by Colin Morris in chronological order:

*Anything but This*, SPCK, 1958
*Nothing to Defend*, Cargate Press, 1959
*The Hour After Midnight*, Longman, 1961
*The End of the Missionary?*, Epworth, 1962
*Out of Africa's Crucible*, Lutterworth, 1963
*Church and Challenge in a New Africa*, Epworth, 1965
*Nationalism in Africa*, SPCK, 1966
*Include Me Out!*, Epworth and Fontana, 1968
*Unyoung, Uncoloured, Unpoor*, Epworth, 1969
*What the Papers Didn't Say*, Epworth, 1971
*The Hammer of the Lord*, Epworth, 1972
*Mankind My Church*, Hodder, 1973
*Epistles to the Apostle*, Hodder, 1975
*The Word and the Words*, Epworth, 1975
*Bugles in the Afternoon*, Epworth, 1977
*Get Through Till Nightfall*, Collins Fontana, 1979
*God-in-a-Box*, Hodder, 1984
*A Week in the Life of God*, Epworth, 1986
*Drawing the Line*, BBC Books, 1987
*Starting from Scratch*, SCM Press, 1990
*Let God be God*, BBC Books, 1991
*Wrestling with an Angel*, Collins, 1992
*Start Your Own Religion*, BBC Books, 1992
*Raising the Dead*, Collins, 1996
*God in the Shower*, Macmillan, 2002
*Bible Reflections Round the Christian Year*, SPCK, 2005

*Things Shaken, Things Unshaken*, Epworth, 2006
*Snapshots*, Epworth, 2007


With Kenneth Kaunda:

*Black Government?*, USPG, 1960
*A Humanist in Africa*, Longman, 1973
*Letter to my Children*, Longman, 1975
*The Riddle of Violence*, Collins, 1980


Other sources:

*Methodist Recorder*
'Neglected Themes in Modern Preaching', address to the Methodist Conference
Sermons from Wesley's Pulpit – recordings by Mr Sydney Cole
'Thought for the Day', *Today*, BBC Radio 4
'Colin Morris, Modern Missionary', PhD thesis, Doris Laird
*Spark in the Stubble*, Leslie Charlton, Epworth, 1969